WARRIOR

HOW TO FIGHT FOR YOUR FAITH, FAMILY, FINANCES, AND FUTURE

WARRIOR

HOW TO FIGHT FOR YOUR FAITH, FAMILY, FINANCES, AND FUTURE

ED RUSH

Ed Rush & Associates, LLC
P.O. Box 1290
Bonita, CA 91908
619-292-2599
Fax: 619-292-2598
E-mail: book@CalledToVictory.com

Limits of Liability and Disclaimer of Warranty

The author and publisher shall not be liable for your misuse of this material. This book is for strictly informational and educational purposes.

DISCLAIMER

The views expressed are those of the author and do not reflect the official policy or position of the Department of Defense, the U.S. government, or the U.S. Marine Corps.

Copyright Use and Public Information

Unless otherwise noted, images have been used by permission and are in keeping with public information laws. Please contact the author for questions about copyrights or the use of public information.

DEDICATION

This book is dedicated to two boys...

Jack and Dean

...who at the time of this writing still love toy guns, shooters, soldiers, and cannons.

Thank you for reminding me that at the heart of every boy is a warrior. It's a lesson I needed to learn especially in the midst of business plans and Sky Miles.

May you follow Christ into battle and grow to be ten times the warrior your father ever was.

TABLE OF CONTENTS

To the Reader

WHEN WRITING A book on what it takes to fight the good fight, the ever-present temptation is to act like you are the spiritual equivalent of Superman (or at least Iron Man). That's because believers—me included—become masters at pretending we are oh-so-holy, especially when we know that we are not.

So, let's clear the air right now.

The warrior in this book is not the one *writing* this book. Instead, I will show you Christ, Captain Extraordinaire. He is the King, after all.

As for me, despite my military record, I am far from a hero. The fingers typing these words belong to a body that has participated in the most detestable acts, led by a mind imagining the worst things, with plank-filled eyes that have seen hell itself (and liked what they saw).

My parents told me not to drink, smoke, chew, or run with those who do. I chose instead to do all four. I have secrets I wouldn't dare tell you, but then again, you have secrets, too, don't you?

The great news is, of course, the Good News tells me I am free. And the cross, resurrection, and ascension of Christ did what I could not do for myself: kill sin, make me alive, and give me great power.

And they have done the same for you.

So, let's stop pretending to be superheroes even if only for a moment.

My goal in writing this book is simple. If just one reader (and that reader being you) decides to join the war to fight for your faith, family, finances, and future, then the world will change and the gates of hell will tremble.

So let's take a good, hard look at Christ the Victor to see how he fought. Then, let's join him in battle for the big win.

SECTION 1:

YOU ARE CALLED TO FIGHT

SECTION 1:
YOU ARE CALLED TO FIGHT

"Christians generally do not believe that God in his providence designed the mind of man for the purpose of man's taking dominion. They do not believe that regenerate minds that necessarily possess 'the mind of Christ' (1 Corinthians 2:16) and are dominically superior to unregenerate minds that have the mind of Satan. Thus, Christians have retreated time and again in cultural and intellectual battles. They have justified these repeated retreats by devising eschatologies of inevitable, guaranteed defeat for the visible kingdom of God. This makes it easier to run up the white flag.

"What else could we expect but defeat? After all, we're Christians."[1]

— Gary North

"What will you do without your freedom?"[2]

— William Wallace, *Braveheart*

"Fight the good fight."

— 1 Timothy 6:12

---

1   Gary North, *Liberating Planet Earth* (Waterbury Center, VT: Dominion Press, 1987), 141.

2   *Braveheart*, directed by Mel Gibson (London, UK: Icon Entertainment, 1995).

O N A HOT afternoon in July 2005, I launched into combat for the first time in an F-18 fighter jet in the skies over Iraq. Having trained for almost ten years, I was now about to face the enemy.

I was—in a word—*terrified*.

I know, I know. As a Marine pilot, I am not supposed to admit fear. But you could describe that particular afternoon as a strange mix of excitement, anticipation, and dread. Combine the excitement of a seven-year-old's birthday party, the anticipation of a groom as the music changes to *Here Comes the Bride*, and the dread of looking off a 10,000-foot ledge knowing you're about to rappel it.

It was all there in some strange, unholy combination of battling emotions, and I did a pretty good job hiding it.

A few hours before the flight, my crew and I went over the details. Our mission was to support an Army forward air controller in the suburbs of Baghdad. Tempers had been flaring recently, and we might need to fight.

We "geared up" about an hour before the flight. I put on my g-suit first. That protects you from blacking out under the extreme g-forces typically experienced in an F-18. I strapped on my torso harness second. It connects the pilot to the parachute and the ejection seat. I put on my Beretta 9-millimeter pistol third. Sliding in a magazine of bullets, I placed it into a holster next to my left rib cage. I was hoping I wouldn't have to use the gun, but I would if it came to that. I put on my survival vest fourth—fifteen pounds of gear to include water, flares, a compass, maps, and even some chewing gum.

I felt the anticipation growing as I walked to the airplane. There was no turning back—I was fully committed. The guys on the ground needed me that day, and my wingman needed me too.

At our undisclosed airbase, I took the runway at approximately 2:05 p.m. Iraq time. And, like a whiteboard eraser, all my fears faded as I set my jaw and focused on the mission.

It was go time.

I lit the afterburners on my two engines and unleashed 36,000 pounds of thrust. My plane catapulted down the runway. Once I hit 160 miles per hour, I pulled the nose up but only slightly. I wanted to be as low as possible so I could avoid detection by enemy surface-to-air missiles. At 350 miles an hour and about ten feet above the runway, I aggressively pulled my airplane into a steep climb. I then dropped the left wing and looked behind me.

No sign of missiles.

As I quickly passed through 10,000 feet, I realized I'd made it. Now it was time for the real mission to begin.

The rest of the flight went as planned. We provided the much-needed air cover. The landing was uneventful—and as I taxied the airplane back to the hangar, I felt a wave of relief hit me. *I'm back. I made it. I'm alive.*

With my first combat mission under my belt, I headed off to the chow hall for a burger and a Red Bull.

Now, fast-forward just one month...

Again, I was in my F-18. Again, I was over the ground of Iraq. And, again, I was in the same piece of sky where the enemy's weapons were aimed to shoot at planes like mine.

Only this time, the emotional mix was much, much different. Excitement was gone. So was anticipation. And fear was *long* gone. In their place was one very different emotion altogether—apathy. Some call it routine.

What was once the most frightening activity of my life had suddenly become a normal part of everyday business in Iraq. Now, mind you, the enemy was still there. They still had the ability to shoot me. And they were still taking shots. It's just that I had flown in this war so many times, I was plain used to it.

In fact, the really scary thing was I flew this mission so many times I almost forgot about the enemy altogether. It was right then I realized the biggest threat to my existence was not the enemy; it was my core belief there *was no enemy.* Even though I knew they were there, I acted like they were not.

The situation could not be more similar for the Christian church today.

First, we fight valiantly against our common enemy. Then, we get used to the fight and the battle becomes routine. Then, the yearly budget, the summer's vacation bible school staffing, and the quarterly picnic become very important (and very distracting).

The next thing you know, the enemy becomes nothing more than a myth.

And the war? Well, that might be something the missionaries in Africa and New Guinea worry about but not the local church. The bake sale is next week—and Martha is distracted with much serving.

The truth is there is a war. There are many battles. Christ is the Captain. You are the weapon. The gates of hell will not win. You will.

That being said, victory and freedom are available for *every* believer. And contrary to what you have been told, the call to a victorious life is not limited *only* to the victory over sin. To choose to ignore the real fight or, worse, to choose *not* to fight will result in the obvious outcome: frustration, failure, and purposelessness. Christ has come that we might have life—and have it to the full—and this kind of "eternal life" is meant for the here and now as much as in eternity.

But to get the victory, you are going to have to fight for it.

This book is a call to action. It is a call to take up arms and join the war. It's a call to rise up as men and women and to fight well. So throughout the pages of this book, we will look at *one* warrior. His name is Jesus Christ, and he is our example as much as he is our King.

Christ conquered enemies, elements, endurance, and even the evil one himself.

And because he conquered, you can too.

But sadly, instead of raising great warriors, the modern version of comfortable Christianity often kills the warrior God birthed inside us. The result has been to spawn a generation of Christian wimps. We don't fight for our families, our faith, our finances, our freedom, our kingdom, our cause, or our God. And because we don't fight, we lose.

It's time for all that to change.

In the movie *Braveheart*, William Wallace spoke to an army in retreat at Striling, Scotland. The dialogue is stirring.

> *William:* You have come to fight as free men. And free man you are! What will you do without freedom? Will you fight?

> *Scottish soldier:* Fight against that? No, we will run, and we will live.

> *William:* Aye, fight and you may die, run and you'll live. At least a while. And dying in your beds many years from now, would you be willing to trade all the days from this day to that for one chance, just one chance to come back here and tell our enemies

that they may take our lives, but they'll never take our freedom!"[3]

Much like William Wallace, we fight because God has given us something *to fight for.* We have been given a true Kingdom (a concept we will explore in a few pages). We are seated with Christ at God's right hand in glory. And we rule and reign with him. Thus, the God of Ages and the Kingdom of Heaven wait for us to crush evil and claim a final victory.

The future of the entire world rests in your answer to this one question:

Will you fight?

If you run, you'll live (for a while). But if you fight, you will win.

This book is about what it takes to win.

---

3   Ibid.

CHAPTER 1:
WHY WE FIGHT

O N JANUARY 17, 1991, a coalition of Allied countries engaged in the greatest display of air power the world had ever seen. The official mission, "Operation Desert Storm," included 100,000 flights and more than 177 million pounds of explosive bombs.[4]

The air war started with unmanned Tomahawk missiles directed at strategic military targets and communication nodes. Soon thereafter followed stealth aircraft—an up-until-then secret

---

4   http://en.wikipedia.org/wiki/Gulf_War_air_campaign

project. Behind the stealth fighters flew aircraft specifically designed to take out the enemy's radar. Those planes cleared the way for the rest of the fighters, bombers, and helicopters.

In the face of imminent destruction, Iraqi leader Saddam Hussein seemed unmoved and unshaken. Five hours after the attacks began, he declared on state radio the following: "The great duel, *the mother of all battles* has begun. The dawn of victory nears as this great showdown begins."[5]

I can remember laughing, literally. This man strutted his pride while bombs exploded in the background. All I could think was, *This guy is going down.*

The truth is, he did go down. It just took twelve years.

Why did it take so long? In 1991, we beat back the Iraqi forces and liberated Kuwait in only a few days. Why, then, did it take another decade to bring down Hussein? Why couldn't air power alone win the war?

The answer is this: *to win a war you must win the ground.*

In 1991, we won the air. In 2003, we won the ground.

Every war is essentially a conflict of *displacement.* You gain ground; the enemy loses ground. When you gain enough ground, the enemy has nowhere to go and they either surrender or die.

For example, in the American Revolutionary War, the British pressed the Continental Army all the way back to Valley Forge. Refitted and reenergized after a long winter, the young American forces surged until the British were pinned down at

---

5   Ibid.

Yorktown. Surrounded by the Continental Army by land and the French Navy by sea, British General Cornwallis surrendered. And a new nation was born.

Later during World War II, the Americans and British went east through France into Germany and the Russians went west. The Allied forces met in Berlin. Once the Allies owned the ground, the war was over.

And so it stands to reason that if we Christians are still fighting this war (some 2,000 years after Christ ascended), then there is still some ground to gain before this conflict is over.

As we begin our discussion of the war you are in, it makes sense to talk about what, exactly, you are fighting for. Just take one glance at the human condition, and you can easily see we all fight. The vital difference between those who fight with honor and those who fight with dishonor is in the objective: the ground. In general, you will either fight for *something* or you will fight against it. You will either fight for *someone* or you will fight against *someone.*

We get this backward all too often. For example, many Christians spend the majority of their time fighting *against* their spouses instead of *for* their spouses. Many believers fight and squabble *against* their church over the smallest doctrinal issues, and yet they rarely ever fight *for* their church.

There are big men and small men; there are big missions and small missions; and there is a big picture and a small picture. You have been called to be a big man and to fight big missions in the big picture.

The small mission to Christianity is frustration, loss, pain, suffering, and discouragement. If you live in this world, you will have difficult times. That is a given. But suffering is never, ever supposed to be a permanent state for the believer. It occurs, but when it does, your job is simple: fight for a breakthrough.

That's because the *big* mission to Christianity is freedom, joy, rest, and peace.

The problem is most Christians remain stuck in the small mission because we embrace it as our *true* Christian calling. Suffering is wrongly held aloft as the *single* virtue that makes us most like Christ.

How appealing.

"Hey, Joe, want to come to my church? Maybe you can even become a Christian and get baptized. All this basically means your really pleasant life is going to go down the drain. Get ready for some suffering, pal! The service is at 11:00. Bring the kids."

The biblical message of victory actually sounds like this:

For *freedom* Christ has set us free; stand firm therefore, and do not submit again to a yoke of slavery. (Galatians 5:1, emphasis mine)

Now the Lord is the Spirit, and where the Spirit of the Lord is, there is *freedom*. (2 Corinthians 3:17, emphasis mine)

The Bible is clear on the major mission: there is freedom, breakthrough, joy, peace, and rest on the other side of victory.[6]

That's why we fight.

Of course, someone will ask, "But didn't Christ suffer?"

Yes, precisely, Christ did suffer. But when you look at why he suffered, you see the big mission: he suffered *for* something greater. The writer of Hebrews says this: "Let us run with endurance the race that is set before us, looking to Jesus, the founder and perfecter of our faith, *who for the joy that was set before him* endured the cross, despising the shame, and is seated at the right hand of the throne of God" (Hebrews 12:1–2, emphasis mine).

Christ suffered *for* something—he suffered *for* the joy of redeeming *everything*. It's so contradictory to our desire for ease that we miss the whole point. Christ endured so he might win an inheritance of nations. He became poor so he might become the richest man in the universe. He fought the small mission to win the big mission.

Now he owns everything—twice. First, he created it and then he redeemed it.

---

6   These two verses are commonly quoted to show Christians how to have victory over sin. That application is correct but limited. I believe a much greater application is found here. The freedom in Scripture is rarely limited only to freedom from sin. It is also a freedom that comes on the other side of fighting and endurance—a freedom that means peace, rest, joy, and life. Sin is but one aspect of many. Christ said he came to bring life, and while freedom from sin is one aspect of life, it is certainly not the only aspect.

Christ fought for one reason: he fought to win.

And so now it's your turn. When it comes to fighting, you can know for whom and what you are supposed to fight by looking at who and what Christ fought for. At a minimum, here are a few ideas:

You fight for your faith (i.e., what you believe).

You fight for the souls of men.

You fight for those who have no one else to fight for them. The battles range from soup kitchens to legal disputes against Planned Parenthood.

You fight for your spouse.

You fight for your kids.

You fight for your loved ones and friends.

You fight for your finances.

You fight for your time.

You fight for your pastor and your leaders. Prayer, support, and encouragement all come to mind.

Last, but not least, you fight for *everything* you have authority over. We'll discuss authority in section 4, but needless to say, authority covers family, work, finances, church, business, employment, property, and recreation. Authority is everything when it comes to fighting, and you have a lot of God-given power to fight in this realm.

To the victor go the spoils. Just look at our King.

Christ fought the battles he chose and on the ground he chose. He fought sin, hunger, and the devil while in the wilderness. He battled the weather and a legion of demons to save one man. He battled an entire Jewish mob to clean up a temple for worship. He battled in the garden, struggling to hold onto the very thing he wanted to let go. He battled in that same garden for the heart of Peter, who would fall, but whom Christ prayed would be restored. He battled at the Cross, tongue clinging to the roof of his mouth, head throbbing, hands numb, barely breathing, and struggling for air. And yet, still grabbing enough air, just enough, he battled to lead a criminal into Paradise.

Christ our Victor. Christ our Captain. Christ our Commander.

He fought well. He fought the good fight. He finished the race. And he *still* fights even when we choose to fold the tents, hand in the weapons, and head home.

Because Christ fought well for you, you can fight well for him.

And so, let's take a look at exactly how Christ fought.

CHAPTER 2:

HOW THIS BOOK WAS WRITTEN

ONE OF THE things that drives theologians crazy is that the Bible was not written as a series of cleanly outlined tips and tricks. An entire discipline of spiritual study called Systematic Theology aims at whittling down the Bible into nice, clean bullets points.

- "Do you want to know what the Bible says about faith? Here are five bullet points (with Scripture reference, of course)."

- "Do you want to know what the Bible says about baptism? Here are five more points."

The problem with this approach is that the Bible was not written this way. It reads more like a conversation between good friends over a beer.

The Bible was written as a story.

So, we make a huge mistake when we come to the Bible first for theology. Instead, we must read the Word of God first as *history* then as theology. We receive the principles out of the story.[7]

And so as we come to the content in this book, it would be quite tempting for me to simply lay out a series of principles on how to wage the spiritual war—something like a three-point outline along with a few clever illustrations.

I will instead draw the points of warfare out of the life of the single greatest warrior in history—namely Christ the Lord. By understanding his story, I think we will find the encouragement we need to live our story.

My goal is to unpack the "warrior themes" in each of the gospels that will help us understand our own battles.

In Matthew, the warrior theme is Christ the King.

In Mark, the warrior theme is Mission.

In Luke, the warrior theme is Authority and Power.

In John, the warrior theme is Timing.

---

7   For a much broader discussion on the importance of reading the Bible as a story, read *Epic* by John Eldredge and *Telling the Truth: The Gospel as Tragedy, Comedy, and Fairy Tale* by Frederick Buechner.

Throughout the Gospels, the warrior theme is How to Endure Suffering.

Then, we will conclude where the Bible concludes: in the book of Revelation where the theme is Christ the Conqueror and You the Victor.

Let's get started.

SECTION 2:

CHRIST THE WARRIOR KING

SECTION 2:
CHRIST THE WARRIOR KING

"The whole point of the…Gospel is, of course, that he is the king in spite of everything. The frog turns out to be the prince, the ugly duckling the swan, the little gray man who asks for bread the great magician with the power of life and death in his hands. And though the steadfast tin soldier falls into the flames, his love turns out to be fireproof."[8]

— Frederick Buechner

"Then shall the King say unto them on his right hand, Come, ye blessed of my Father, inherit the kingdom *prepared for you* from the foundation of the world."

— Matthew 25:34 KJV (emphasis mine)

8   Frederick Buechner, *Telling the Truth: The Gospel as Tragedy, Comedy, and Fairy Tale* (New York, NY: Harper Collins, 1977), 90.

THE LEGEND OF Robin Hood is about a man devoted to the *true* king and similarly opposed to the *false* one. While King Richard the Lionhearted was off fighting wars and making alliances, his brother, the evil Prince John, usurped the throne and went about acting as if the king would never return.

Against all odds, Robin and his band of merry men courageously provided help where there was none. They interceded for the people and against tyranny. And they lived long enough to see the real king come back home.

> Robin Hood looked our comely king intently in the face; Sir Richard at the Lee did likewise and they both now recognized their lord king. Outlaw and knight both kneeled before him; and when those wild outlaws saw their leader kneel, so too did they sink to their knees before their king.
>
> "My lord, the king of England!" exclaimed Robin.

"Then I must ask you mercy...Robin, of your goodness and your grace for my men and me," said the king.

"I grant it and God save me, my lord King," said Robin. "I ask mercy and a pardon for all my men and me."

"Yes, I grant it, for that is the reason I came to the greenwood," said the king. "But you and your men must leave the greenwood and come to live with me at court."[9]

At the end of the story, the enemy was defeated, the kingdom was restored, and Robin and his men moved to the court of the king, never to want for the rest of their lives.

Sure, it's a fairy tale, but the reason why this story (among others) has stood the test of time is it so accurately mirrors our own story. That's because when the true King comes, we have only one correct choice: we fall on our faces and *serve* him.

As we make our way through the Gospels, our first stop is the book of Matthew. The former tax collector wrote his gospel account for first-century Jews. Matthews's main concern was to announce the coming of the true King. In fact, the theme of the coming King is so prevalent Matthew uses the term "kingdom of heaven" thirty-two times in twenty-eight chapters.

---

9   http://myweb.tiscali.co.uk/sherwoodtimes/richardm.htm

That single phrase "the kingdom of heaven" is the key to understanding the whole Gospel of Matthew, and it's a wonder how we've got it so wrong.

Honestly, what does the average person think of when he hears the term "kingdom of heaven"? Ask a man on his way out of church. He will probably say something about clouds, angels, harps, and maybe Peter and his front-gate patrol.

In other words, it's very far away and perhaps not too concerned with what you had for breakfast this morning.

Dallas Willard writes,

The damage done to our practical faith in Christ and in his government-at-hand by confusing heaven with a place in distant or outer space, or even beyond space, is incalculable. Of course, God is there too. But instead of heaven and God also being always present with us, as Jesus shows them to be, we invariably take them to be located far away and, most likely, at a much later time—not here and not now. And we should be surprised to feel ourselves alone.[10]

Contrary to the common man and his opinions, Jesus had something different in mind altogether when he spoke of the kingdom of heaven. He had in mind an invasion force ready for a fight. He had in mind the power that was his and the same power that was going to be ours. He had in mind an

---

10   Dallas Willard, *The Divine Conspiracy* (New York, NY: Harper Collins, 1998), 71.

all-out assault from heaven to the earth, neither to be the same ever again. He had in mind Emmanuel—GOD WITH US—now and for the rest of this week, month, and year.

The kingdom of heaven, in short, was to be the real tangible presence of Almighty God spread into all the corners of life, to include family, finances, business, government, the arts, and even to the nick on your cheek from shaving this morning.

It's not coming later and certainly not *much* later. We don't have to wait for the fulfillment of some obscure prophesy for the Kingdom to come. The Kingdom *has* come and the Kingdom is *still* coming. It's been here for a while and it's planning on staying, thank you very much.

In the very first pages of Matthew, we hear about the Kingdom from John the Baptist, who was sent as an ambassador to prepare the way for the King: "In those days John the Baptist came preaching in the wilderness of Judea, 'Repent, for *the kingdom of heaven is at hand*'" (Matthew 3:1–2, emphasis mine).

And then to make sure we don't miss the message, Christ comes back in the next chapter to remind us things are about to change, now that the new Sheriff is in town. "From that time Jesus began to preach, saying, 'Repent, for the *kingdom of heaven is at hand*'" (Matthew 4:17, emphasis mine).

Over the next three years, Jesus compared the kingdom of heaven to a sown seed, to a grain of mustard, to yeast expanding in bread, to good seed plowed in a field, to a treasure found in a field, to a merchant finding expensive pearls, to a net pulling in fish, to a king asking about his property, and to ten virgins waiting and waiting and waiting for the groom. (Matthew 13:24, 31, 33, 38, 44, 45, 47; 20:1; 25:1).

In other words, the Kingdom is so fierce no one can stop it, and when it gets here, it's going to be very, very good.

Jesus told his disciples the kingdom of heaven was something to pray for, fight for, prepare for, and strive for (Matthew 6:13; 7:21; 11:12; 19:14).

He also said that in the kingdom of heaven, you get glory, reward, and one heck of a dinner (Matthew 5:10; 8:10; 13:43).

Oh and last, but certainly not least, the kingdom of heaven is something you inherit personally after you have fought well and prevailed: "Then shall the King say unto them on his right hand, Come, ye blessed of my Father, inherit the kingdom *prepared for you* from the foundation of the world" (Matthew 25:34 KJV).

Think about receiving Warren Buffet's inheritance, then multiplying it by...infinity.

R. J. Rushdoony puts it this way, "The salvation of man includes his restoration into the image of God and the calling implicit in that image, to subdue the earth and to exercise dominion. Hence, the proclamation of the gospel was also the proclamation of the Kingdom of God."[11]

---

11   R. J. Rushdoony, *Institutes of Biblical Law* (Phillipsburg, NJ: P & R Publishing, 1980), 449.

Let there be no mistake. The announcement of the gospel *is* the announcement of the coming King. Jesus did not come to earth only to make a personal connection with you. He didn't come *just* to save you from your sins. And he didn't come just so that we could all hold hands around the campfire singing, "Jesus loves me; this I know, for the Bible tells me so."

He did all of that and so much more. He came to restore *all* things, to win *all* things, and to conquer *all* things.

In other words, he came to reign.

So now that we know what the Kingdom is, the obvious question to ask is what exactly you are supposed to do about it. The answer is threefold: you recognize it, you receive it, and then you stand up as a man and fight for it.

CHAPTER 3:
RECOGNIZING
THE KINGDOM

SOMEWHERE AMONGST TINSEL, trinkets, and toys, we have completely lost the Christmas story. It's not Santa Claus's fault, so don't blame him. Don't blame Macy's either. We lost Christmas long before Old Saint Nick and Cabbage Patch dolls.

For example, just answer this one question: how many wise men visited Jesus? Fill in the blanks, "We ___ Kings of Orient are, bearing gifts we travelled so far..."

Three, right?

Wrong.

The Bible never says how many wise men there were. And it definitely doesn't say three. That number has been passed down most likely because there were three gifts brought to Jesus (gold, frankincense, and myrrh). It's only one example among many errors in our modern view of the incarnation of Christ. And because we lost the *details* in the Christmas story, we lost a lot of the *power* of the story as well.

So what is the real story of the wise men? Here goes: it took about a year of traveling for these men "from the east" to get to Jerusalem. They carried piles of gold in their caravan. (It was the most precious commodity in that day just like it is in ours.) These men were obviously very influential—most likely they were counselors to kings—famed astronomers usually were.

Now, let me ask you this. Do highly influential men carrying gobs of gold travel across the Arabian Desert alone?

Nope. They bring a train of servants, supplies, and armed guards. In other words, this was a big caravan. It most likely had a lot of people and wielded a lot of power.

Here is what Matthew tell us, "Now after Jesus was born in Bethlehem of Judea in the days of Herod the king, behold, wise men from the east came to Jerusalem, saying, 'Where is he who has been born king of the Jews? For we saw his star when it rose and have come to worship him.' When Herod the king heard this, he was troubled, and all Jerusalem with him" (Matthew 2:1–3).

Is it possible for three simple travelers to trouble "all Jerusalem"? No. This caravan was big enough to get the capital city's attention. And what the wise men said to Herod was an even bigger deal. You see, Herod was one of the most evil and vindictive rulers in the history of Israel. No one—and I mean no one—got in his way. So, as you might imagine, this message about the newborn "king of the Jews" bothered Herod...just a little bit. That's because Herod fashioned himself as the real king of the Jews, and to make matters worse he didn't have any baby sons in the house.

So Herod got some smart Jewish scholars together for a little discussion about the coming Messiah. Here is what he asked them, "and assembling all the chief priests and scribes of the people, he inquired of them where the Christ was to be born. They told him, 'In Bethlehem of Judea'" (Matthew 2:4–5).

These were strange bedfellows indeed—Herod (the local representative of Caesar) and the Jewish leaders (who hated Caesar)—all together as one happy family.

You know the rest of the story. Herod sent the wise men off to find Christ. When they didn't return, he sent his soldiers into Bethlehem to kill every child under two years old. Jesus, Mary, and Joseph escaped but just barely. Herod later died. Jesus lived, died, *and rose again* to earn an inheritance of nations. The King of the Jews became the King of Everything, and Herod went down in the books as one of history's biggest losers. (Don't you just love happy endings?)

OK, now stop for a moment and go back to the scene at Herod's palace. There is something strange that occurred, and we need to look at it for a moment.

What do we know? We know there was a star—an out-of-the-ordinary astronomical sign. We know that these very wise astronomers traveled a very long time to visit a new king, apparently because they believed God told them to do so. We also know the Messiah was to be born in Bethlehem—the Jewish leaders told Herod that much. And we also know Jesus was born in Bethlehem—at exactly the same time the Messiah was *supposed to be born.*

But what is so remarkable about this story is not what is there but *what is missing.* Despite *all* of the facts, Herod sent an invasion force, and the Jewish leaders apparently went home for a warm bowl of soup.

Now, considering everything they knew, what should they have done?

Answer: Herod should have realized God was in charge, and he should have gone to worship the Messiah.

Answer: The Jewish leaders should have welcomed Jesus as their true King.

Herod was a megalomaniac at this point, and he couldn't help himself. Instead of worship, he attacked.

The Jewish leaders were truly without excuse. They were so concerned with the opinions of Herod and of their place at the table, that they dismissed Christ all together—even after telling Herod the correct address for the birth of the Messiah. They could have at least paid Jesus a little visit. Heck, if they had, just like the wise men, they would have even ended up in the Community Church's Annual Living Manger Scene.

Instead, the Jewish leaders did...nothing! Their actions are remarkable only in their absence.

Sadly, the same is true for the church today.

Our primary responsibility as spiritual warriors is to *fight* for the Kingdom. And step number one is *recognizing* that the Kingdom *has* come.

We do this, first, by doing the very opposite of what Herod did. Instead of fighting *against* God, we should fight *with* him. We give up demanding our creature comforts and get in the spiritual foxhole.

Herod wanted to keep his kingdom intact. He had a comfortable position at the top of the Palestinian food chain, and he was intent on keeping it. We make fun of Herod until we realize we have it pretty good too. Food, comfort, peace, rest, and on-demand movies. Three square meals a day and complimentary Wi-Fi. Our lives (mine included) can often be described as wholly selfish.

Think about it: if Herod were to visit the average twenty-first-century American home, he would give up his entire first-century kingdom to stay here.

See the shock on Herod's face as he tours your home.

Wait a second. You pull this lever and fresh water just comes out? When does it stop? Never??

And there's even more water over here. Hmm, that looks fresh too. How does it taste? What...you pee in the clean water? You have got to be kidding me!

We have it pretty good, don't we?

Honestly, how much of your life is spent doing only what you want to do, despite the fact you know better? (It breaks my heart as I answer this question for myself.) How much of your life is spent for the sole purpose of comfort or convenience? And just so you know, this is not a call to a navel-gazing, self-centric Christian guilt-trip. It's a wakeup call. There is a world around you that needs some help.

And the Kingdom *has* come.

The first step in recognizing the Kingdom is nothing more than a step of *awareness*. You simply open your eyes to the world around you and ask the simple question, "What would it take here to see God's will be done?" Sometimes it is as simple as a prayer, a word of encouragement, a smile, a hug, or a dollar bill. Sometimes it takes rolling up your sleeves and getting dirty. Sometimes it means a complete change of lifestyle and mission.

It all starts with opening your eyes so you can move out of "the kingdom of me" and into the "kingdom of heaven." Herod refused to do that, and he lost in the end. The good news is, it is not too late for you and me.

In the *second* place, recognizing Christ's kingdom is to do the very opposite thing the Jewish leaders did. Frankly, they should have known better, but they were far too comfortable to do anything risky. The very act of worshipping the newborn

King would have led to their losing prestige and power. That wasn't going to happen anytime soon. Therefore worship was not an option.

So, as baby Jesus fled for his life, the religious elite sat in Jerusalem on their comfy couches watching late-night reruns of *Leave It to Beaver*.

Unlike the Jewish leaders, recognizing the Kingdom means to worship with no strings attached. It means to give up *anything* we love more than Christ. It means to give up the right to prestige and power.

Ask yourself: *is there anything in my life I would not be willing to give up to see God's Kingdom come?*

Pause for a moment and answer that question.

Whatever just came to mind, that is your idol.

It could be your home, car, 401K, Jet Ski, cigar collection, or just your backyard grill. It could be your kid's baseball swing, your smile, your reputation, or your blog. (My personal list is pretty long.)

Now take the thing you just thought of and say,

God, I give this to you. Take it away if you need to. If not, please give it back sanctified so I may use it for you.

If you can't pray that prayer (and sometimes we can't), simply ask God to give you the *heart* to be able to pray that prayer.

Here is what I just prayed for: this book.

You see, I have very mixed motives for this book. Part of me wants this message to change the world for the Kingdom.

I want to see men (and women) arise and fight for their faith, family, and finances. I want to see a generation of Christian wimps transformed into a generation of Christian warriors.

I want this with all of my heart.

However there is also another motive that has crept in recently like a slithering sidewinder. You see, only three days ago, I gave a chapter of this book to my friend and pastor. I wanted to get his thoughts on "how I was doing." Honestly, I really did want his feedback.

But secretly, I also wanted something else. I wanted him to say I am the smartest man alive, that the book is awesome and I should expect a coronation sometime soon.

[Sigh.]

It seems there is no end to our desire to make idols.[12] So, here is what I just prayed,

> God, I give you this book and I give you the desire for
> man's approval. I am yours and so is this book. Do
> with me (and it) what you want to do. Take it away
> if you want to. And if you give it back, please give it

---

12   John Calvin wrote that the human heart was a "perpetual factory
      of idols." That's pretty true; but then again Christ came to rule,
      and part of what he intends to rule is your heart. I have personally
      fought the idol of "pride" for a long time. I still do. But what I have
      noticed is that, by God's design, I am also becoming more whole...and
      therefore, more holy. I guess what I am saying is that there is hope.
      The Heidelberg Catechism says that, "even the holiest men, while in
      this life, have only a small beginning of this obedience." I like the
      Heidelberg Catechism, but I think that line is totally screwed up.
      Christ is the King, and I am pretty sure he can accomplish more than
      just a "small beginning." I think, with your permission, that Christ
      can totally remake you. And that would be remarkable indeed. So,
      just let him, OK?

*back sanctified so it and I may serve you. May your
Kingdom come.*

If you are reading this book, it means God gave this book
back and the "Ed Rush Coronation" got cancelled.

Just feel free to reword that prayer for your particular idol
or issue.

OK, now this is important. Once you have prayed to
release your idols and given them to God, *get back in the
fight.* There is no condemnation and you are forgiven. So stop
feeling guilty and start *fighting.* Repentance is not an excuse for
inactivity. That was the Jewish leader's excuse, not yours. So, in
the absence of any other leading from God, keep fighting!

Last, as we *recognize* the coming of the Kingdom, we see
Christ's incarnation was an all-out assault on the world. But all
too often, instead of going on the attack, we choose to retreat
while singing carols of nonsensical nothingness. Again, let's use
the distortion of the Christmas story as our launching point.
Listen (and sing along) to this familiar song,

Away in a manger,

No crib for His bed

The little Lord Jesus

Laid down His sweet head

The stars in the bright sky

Looked down where He lay

The little Lord Jesus

Asleep on the hay

The cattle are lowing

The poor Baby wakes

But little Lord Jesus

No crying He makes[13]

That has to be the most ridiculous Christmas hymn ever. It's a lie and an absurd distortion of the true story. For heaven's sake, just because Jesus was God doesn't mean he didn't cry. He was all-human, which means he was also *all-baby*.

This is my version of what the manger scene probably looked like. It doesn't rhyme (and I haven't yet set it to music), but at least it's closer to the truth than that other song.

A cow drops a pile of dung in the corner,

Mary rolls over with eyes oh so red

(she's had three hours of sleep in the last two days),

...and Jesus poops in his second-to-last clean diaper.

Joseph has a dream; bolting upright he startles the chickens.

He hurries to wake up everyone and they all run (not walk)

out of town with what they can in their arms.

---

13 "Away in a Manger," *Little Children's Book for Schools and Families*, by J. C. File (Philadelphia, PA: Evangelical Lutheran Church in North America, 1885).

...and Jesus poops in his last clean diaper.[14]

That sounds more like it, right? (A lot of moms are nodding their heads right now). It's a sad, startling, gruesome tale of a family fleeing for their lives. They barely make it and...

A few days later, there is not a boy left alive in Bethlehem under the age of two.

The birth of Christ was an assault on behalf of the kingdom of heaven against the kingdom of this world. This takes me back to my first point. When we lose the details in the story, we lose the meaning of the story. It wasn't about Jesus, meek and mild; it was about Jesus the Warrior-King come to earth.

It was a battle. And it was fiercely opposed.

This point is critical because as you begin giving up your idols expect that to be opposed as well. The thief, Christ tells us, comes to steal, kill, and destroy. As you begin to take back what has been stolen, killed, or destroyed, you can bet your bottom dollar that it will include a fight—just like it did when Christ came.

The good news, of course, is God writes great stories and he loves happy endings. He fought in Bethlehem and he

---

14   The idea for this little carol of mine came from a blog post by John Eldredge called "Jesus had poopie diapers" (www.RansomedHeart. com). All too often, we totally disregard Jesus' humanity because we have the sneaking suspicion that to be human is to be all messed up. Well, Jesus became human without messing up *sinfully*, but that is not to say he didn't mess up his pants every once in a while.

fought on the cross. He won both times. He will fight for you also, which means when you fight together with him you will win too.

Now, here is the paradox: once you *recognize* the Kingdom, your next step is to act like a child.

CHAPTER 4:
RECEIVING THE KINGDOM

JESUS ALWAYS WENT against the grain. I love that about him. Just when his disciples thought they had him all figured out, he always changed strategies on them and left them in the dust.

Such an occasion came just about the time his ministry really got momentum. Jesus had been healing, casting out demons, and multiplying food, and he had an army of followers ready to do whatever he wanted them to do.

Now, it is time to get serious, the apostles probably thought. *He's going to be the King and, of course, we'll have some property and prestige to show for it. So whatever happens, make sure Jesus has the time he needs to prepare the invasion against the Romans. Andrew, Philip, stand guard. John and I need a word with him in private.*

Then the pesky Peterson peasants showed up with their kids Paul and Patricia in tow—snot dripping out of their noses and ragdolls dangling from their grubby little hands. And to make matters worse, these parents had the annoying audacity to ask Jesus to pray for their little urchins.

The disciples wouldn't hear of it. "Then children were brought to him that he might lay his hands on them and pray. The disciples rebuked the people, but Jesus said, 'Let the little children come to me and do not hinder them, for to such belongs the kingdom of heaven.' And he laid his hands on them and went away" (Matthew 19:13–15).

Jesus, in effect, told his loyal followers they had it all wrong...down to the very jot and tittle. That the little ones—the ones who can't even pronounce the name "Jesus" without lisping over the "s"—are the new kings and queens. That they are going to reign with Christ. That the Kingdom is basically going to be run by kids and maybe even some adults who act like kids.

Frederick Buechner says it this way:

And the good ones, the potentially good anyway,
the ones who stand a chance of being saved by
God because they know they don't stand a chance

of being saved by anybody else? They go around looking like the town whore, the village drunk, the crook from the IRS, because they know who they are. When Jesus is asked who is the greatest in the Kingdom of Heaven, he reaches into the crowd and pulls out a child with a cheek full of bubble gum and eyes full of whatever a child's eyes are full of and says unless you can become like that, don't bother to ask.[15]

The gospel is at its core very good news. It is very good news indeed. It means that whatever you were, whatever you've done, and whatever you've become is a thing of the past. Gone. Cancelled. Separated from you as far as east is from west.

It means when you come to Christ as a child, he restores you as a king, giving you a crown, dominion, and a palace.

It's out of this world.

Remember those secrets I mentioned in the introduction to this book—the ones you are desperate to keep from everyone, the same ones I told you I have too? The good news is the kingdom of heaven is made up entirely of people like you and me—people with deep, dark secrets and "eyes full of whatever a child's eyes are full of." God's invasion force is essentially made up of the lame, the weary, the abused, the sick, the tired, and the poor. It's made up of people just like you and me—people who wake up in the morning and wonder, *How am I going to get the strength to make it until the next paycheck?*

15   Buechner, *Telling the Truth*, 89-90.

Now, pause for a moment and think about God's choice of warriors. If *we* were going to war, we would find the strongest soldiers we could get our hands on. When God goes on the assault, he gets a bunch of kids, or at least a bunch of adults who act like kids. He forms them in ranks, gives them the mission, and all that without a backup plan.

The key, of course, is to come out of hiding and run to the King—just like Robin Hood did. Ask him for a full pardon for you and for your men. Next thing you know you'll be swept off your feet, given a battle array, and invited to a feast beyond description.

Oh, the depths of the riches and the wisdom of God.

Now, here is the very exciting part: once you are in the King's presence, you should feel totally free to ask for a lot of things and ask a lot. Those of you who are parents know what kind of asking I am talking about. I have three very ambitious children who are not afraid of asking for everything, and at times all at once. What's the risk? Dad may say no, but then again he may say yes too!

> *Dad, can I go to Disneyland?*
> *Dad, can I watch a movie tonight?*
> *Dad, can I have ice cream for breakfast?*
> *Dad, can I have a spaceship?*

The heart of a child is to ask for things and to ask a lot. So, why does this kind of asking typically end when we get all grown up and serious? Your heavenly Father knows what you need, and at times he gives you what you need, along with a bunch of other things you don't need but just want. He's generous and kind, and he really loves giving good gifts.

Brennan Manning shares a funny account of what it means to ask the King for big things:

> Years ago the professional golfer Arnold Palmer played a series of exhibition matches in Saudi Arabia. When he finished, the king was so impressed with Palmer's expertise that he desired to give Palmer a gift. Palmer, a multimillionaire in his own right, demurred: "It isn't really necessary. I just enjoyed meeting your people and playing in your country." The king indicated his extreme displeasure at not being able to give the golf pro a gift. Palmer wisely reconsidered and said, "Well, how about a golf club? A golf club would be a wonderful memento of my visit here." The king was pleased. The following day, a messenger delivered to Palmer's hotel room the title to a golf club, thirty-six holes, tress, lakes, buildings. The moral of this story? In the presence of the king, don't ask for small gifts.[16]

Let me share with you a fun personal example of asking for and getting things you want but don't really need. I don't know why, but God routinely gives me really great parking spaces. I've come to call this, "Ed Rush Parking." Just the other day, I went to a major league baseball game. The game having already started, I pulled into a full parking lot and asked, "Lord,

---

16   Brennan Manning, *The Furious Longing of God* (Colorado Springs, CO: David C. Cook, 2009), 110–11.

could you give me a spot right up front?" Sure enough, I drove right up to the stadium, and, voilà, right in row number one was a perfect spot waiting for me and for me alone.

This happens more times than I can count. My friends and family just laugh. And honestly I can't explain it. All I can say is God has fun watching me get a good parking spot.

He is so kind. And sometimes he answers our prayers not because we are so good, but because he is so good. So if you are not already asking, start now! Ask for things you don't even need. Ask and ask a lot. Ask for those who don't ask or who can't ask. It is Christ's kingdom after all. You are his child, and you might just be surprised at what you get.

As you grow to maturity as a warrior for the Kingdom, always remember the Kingdom first belongs to kids. So, come to God first as a child, and then ask him to make you a warrior.

The gospel of the kingdom of heaven is the story of a King who has come and one who accepts us as we are, as long as we are willing to shed all pretence and come as a child. After all, that's what Christ did.

CHAPTER 5:
FIGHTING FOR THE KINGDOM

S O, NOW THAT you have come as a child and have asked as a child, it's time to stand up and fight like a man.

One of the most poignant moments in all of Scripture occurred when Jesus got angry. He demonstrated anger only a few times, but when he did, it was well deserved and always without sin.

One such time was when Jesus wreaked absolute havoc on a marketplace in the outer temple. To really understand the situation, you need to know that just outside the main temple area was a three-hundred- to five-hundred-yard-long place called the Court of the Gentiles. Non-Jews and unhealthy Jews were, in fact, welcome to come to the temple, and they were encouraged to worship the true God of Israel. It's just that they were not allowed by law to enter the main temple. That space was reserved for Jews in good standing and in good health.

The inner sanctuary was a quiet worship place for Jews. The outer court was *supposed* to be a quiet worship place for Gentiles. The Jews, however, had a different idea. They decided the Court of the Gentiles was a good place to set up shop. Bulls, goats, pigeons, and money—and lots of it—crowded out the well-meaning non-Jews.

The Jews were, in effect, saying their commerce and convenience was far more important than an outsider's right to pray.

> Jesus was infuriated. "And Jesus entered the temple and drove out all who sold and bought in the temple, and he overturned the tables of the money-changers and the seats of those who sold pigeons. He said to them, 'It is written, "My house shall be called a house of prayer,"' but you make it a den of robbers" (Matthew 21:12–13).

You already know that part of the story—it's pretty famous. Jesus cleaned out the temple. It was total pandemonium. But when we remember that story, we usually picture Jesus then leaving the temple, on to bigger and better things. Matthew, however, says Jesus stayed put for a while. The scene was magnificent. Read and see who came *back* into the Court of the Gentiles to meet with God.

> And the blind and the lame came to him in the temple, and he healed them. But when the chief priests and the scribes saw the wonderful things that he did, and the children crying out in the temple, "Hosanna to the Son of David!" they were indignant, and they said to him, "Do you hear what these are saying?" And Jesus said to them, "Yes; have you never read, 'Out of the mouth of infants and nursing babies you have prepared praise'?" (Matthew 21:14–16)

This is spectacular.

The blind and the lame could not enter the main temple area because...well, because they were blind and lame. There were rules against such things. After Jesus did his house cleaning, the blind and lame came back into the Court of the Gentiles and made a bee-line for Jesus. He promptly healed them, which, in effect, made them fit to worship, not just in the Court of the Gentiles but in the main sanctuary as well.

The overall reaction is hysterical. Children began running around the court singing a song about the coming Messiah—the man right in front of them. They, of course, understood what the Jewish leaders, deprived of their commerce, failed once again to grasp. The King had come with power and he was here to stay.

Then, displaying their true blindness, the Jewish leaders formed ranks to kill Jesus—and all this for showing real Jews what real Jews should have been doing in the first place.

This whole story serves to orient our warrior hearts to the true nature of the battle. We are called to fight *for* those whom Christ fought for. And we are called to fight *against* those whom Christ fought against. We follow our Captain and fight for those whom by virtue of their lot in life cannot fight for themselves. We fight for the orphan by bringing her into our home and making her a daughter. We fight for the pregnant woman by giving her a future. We fight for government leaders who refuse to steal money to fund pensions and pet projects. We fight for the homeless and poor (the real ones at least) by giving them a cup of cold water and a hot meal.

In short, we are called to fight because they have been given so little and because we have been given so much.

The gospel of the kingdom of heaven is the story of a King who turned over tables and whipped merchants to make a way for the lost, the destitute, and the outcast. He did this, first because they had it coming and second because he was showing you what you are supposed to do.

Does it take courage to stand up for the outcast? You bet it does. First, it's inconvenient. Second, it's unpopular.

Honestly, I wish I had more personal examples, but I can quickly think of two.[17] We opened our home up recently to a

---

17   I hesitate to give personal examples of service. To be honest, I could do a w-a-a-a-a-y better job practicing what I preach. Basically, I am pretty selfish (but I am working on it). My wife Bonnie is worlds

homeless woman. To put it mildly, she stunk. But she came to church that morning, and my wife and I felt like we should do something. We gave her two meals, a shower, and a car full of groceries. In the interest of full disclosure, I could have used a nap that afternoon, but, instead, we served. We were given so much, and we wanted to use it for the Kingdom.

I have no idea what happened to that woman or what effect that one day had on her. All I know is we did what we were called to do—to fight for one woman for one day.

Here is a second example: we recently served as "interim" foster parents for a baby girl.[18] She came to us at age two—as in two *days* old. We cared for her (which pretty much means we fed her, changed her, and prayed for her) for six weeks until the agency found the right adoptive family. Between us, that was a pretty inconvenient six weeks. We missed date nights, movie nights, and lost a lot of sleep. To be fair, I was out of town speaking about half of the time. My wife, Bonnie, did the hard work. Even with all that, I'll bet you that little girl will never

---

better at this than me, and she has taught me a lot. Anyway, my point is that you shouldn't read what I am writing about service and feel all bad about yourself. I am not a super hero (a fact that you should be aware of by now). Just serve and let Jesus do the rest.

18   "Interim foster care" basically means providing a home while a child is in the adoptive process. In a perfect world, the birth mom chooses an adoptive family before the child is born. It's not a perfect world, so there are "surprises." Instead of the state then taking care of the child, some adoption agencies have families on call (like ours) who are ready to provide a home. The agency we work with is Bethany Christian Services, www.bethany.org.

even know our names. We didn't do it for the recognition; we did it because we have been given so much, and we wanted to use it for the Kingdom.

OK, so now it's your turn.

What is Christ asking you to fight for? *Who* is Christ asking you to fight for? My guess is someone or something just popped into your mind. Perhaps it's a deliverance ministry against abortion, a hospitality ministry for the (real) homeless, an arts ministry for the local town, or a financial stewardship ministry for your church members. Maybe it's a person: a long-lost family member, a beleaguered co-worker, or the guy who mows your lawn. A lot of need is in the world today, which means the examples could be endless. Just take a few minutes to ask God what/who he would have you fight for.

Then, get in the fight.

CHAPTER 6:
THE KINGDOM THAT IS STILL COMING

THE LAST POINT we'll discuss about the Kingdom is that it is both a kingdom that has come and one *still* coming. Frankly, that sounds like a contradiction.

"Honey, is Sam home from school yet?"

"Yes, dear, he is home."

"Can I talk to him?"

"Well, he's kinda home and he's kinda still coming home?"

Wh-a-a-a-t?

The idea the Kingdom has come and is still coming is difficult to understand unless you put it into a military context (which of course is perfect because, after all, this is a war).

The World War II battle for Okinawa (June 1945) claimed an estimated 62,000 American lives and 95,000 Japanese lives. Due to the fact the victory occurred on the Japanese homeland, it was, by all estimates, the defining battle that spelled the end of Imperial Japan.[19]

Three months and two bombs later on September 2, 1945, U.S. officers accepted the unconditional surrender of Japanese armed forces. It was the official end of hostilities. By God's grace, both the United States and Japan grew into industrial powerhouses and eventually became good friends and allies.

But you'll never guess when World War II fighting *actually* ended.

April 1980.

That was the day Captain Fumio Nakahira of the Japanese Imperial Army surrendered. Apparently he held out in a cave at Mt. Halcon, Philippines, for 35 years before being discovered.[20] As we say in the Marines, "There is always someone who doesn't get the word."

That analogy perfectly fits our current situation, and here is why.

Christ came to land the decisive blow. The victory is now secure. Christ's kingdom is here and he has won. And yet there

---

19   http://en.wikipedia.org/wiki/Battle_of_Okinawa

20   http://www.wanpela.com/holdouts/list.html

are still pockets of resistance stubbornly refusing to give up the ground and to allow us to take dominion over what is rightfully ours. During this time of siege, the church (that's you and me) is the military force of Christ that is intended to secure the final victory.

Back in chapter 1, I mentioned all wars are won by securing the ground—the infantry must get a foothold and gain land. And that is exactly what is happening in the spiritual war we fight today.

Paul puts it this way: "Then comes the end, when he delivers the kingdom to God the Father after destroying every rule and every authority and power. *For he must reign until he has put all his enemies under his feet*" (1 Corinthians 15:24–25, emphasis mine).

The story of Christ's final and ultimate victory is a story of his reigning until he puts all enemies to death—the last enemy being death itself.

The sad news is the church has failed to realize this one point for so long we have actually *lost* ground. The defeated enemy has not only kicked us out of Okinawa but out of Midway and Iwo Jima as well! They have done that precisely because the church has *chosen* to believe the lie that we are semi-defeated in this world, and, therefore, we must wait for some future heaven, rapture, or second coming for all of this to become a reality.

Christians are called to rule in every area of society. But instead of ruling, we submit ourselves to ungodly rulers and hang on tight until Sunday. You see this in almost every sphere of culture. Take, for instance, movies, art, business, and books. Had Christians been doing what Christians *should* have been doing, just about every great movie today would be written by Christian writers. The latest ballet would feature a redemptive theme and feature believing dancers. The top 400 of the Forbes richest men would *all* be Christians.[21] And Christians would pen the best-selling books.

But instead of taking dominion, we verbally rail against culture while at the same time providing no suitable alternative.

Let me give you a few examples.

I attended a church one Sunday where the pastor said this, "Well, such-and-such told me he was a Christian, but then I saw him walking into a movie theater. And we all know Christians shouldn't do that!"

Seriously, where does the Bible say we shouldn't watch movies?

How about this? Instead of complaining *against* the evils of current movies, why not start writing decidedly excellent, decidedly Christian movies?

---

21 Proverbs 13:22 says that, "the sinner's wealth is laid up for the righteous." The biblical pattern of money transfer should be from nonbelievers to believers. That's because we are called to take dominion of the world's wealth both honestly and ethically—and money is only one small part of dominion. This concept has been so lost on the Christian church that, instead of taking dominion, we vilify people with money. That's not Christianity; that's socialism. I am particularly thankful for my friend Steven DeSilva. He wrote the book that I was going to write about money (and did a much better job of it). It's called *Money and the Prosperous Soul*, and you should read it.

Thank God for churches like Sherwood Baptist Church of Albany, Georgia, and Alex Kendrick, the church's minister of media. They are the driving force behind the movie *Fireproof* and other Christian movies, such as *Flywheel* and *Facing the Giants.* Thank God for Mel Gibson, who produced *The Passion of the Christ.* (Boy, did he get a lot of flack from the "evangelical elite" for that movie.)

During the 1980s, the church at large condemned rock and roll as "the devil's instrument." Congregations gathered all over the world to listen to Def Leopard songs played backward, hoping to hear some kind of satanic message to prove their point. Not coincidentally, at the same time, Christian rock and roll was downright horrible. I remember buying a few tapes back then—just to make myself feel better about my robust non-Christian music collection. I couldn't even follow the beat. And no wonder. With all the accusations about the nature of rock and roll, would *you* have wanted to be a Christian artist back then?

Instead of endless debates about which music style is most "God-honoring," why not encourage young gifted believers to write and play decidedly good Christian music—or for that matter, just good music written by Christians.

Instead of discussions as to whether or not "dancing is of the devil," why not write Christian ballets? It would be a pleasant change to the clearly non-redemptive ending of ballets such as *Swan Lake.* My seven-year-old daughter is a whiz at ballet. How great would it be if she could join a ballet company that clearly had Christ as its King?

Instead of debating whether oil companies should be allowed to "profit," why not establish companies with decidedly Christian values. Take, for example, Chick-fil-A, which chooses to forgo at least one seventh of all of its profits by closing its doors on Sunday. This is from the company's website: "Our founder, Truett Cathy, made the decision to close on Sundays in 1946 when he opened his first restaurant in Hapeville, Georgia. He has often shared that his decision was as much practical as spiritual. He believes that all franchised Chick-fil-A operators and their restaurant employees should have an opportunity to rest, spend time with family and friends, and worship if they choose to do so."[22]

Now that's called taking dominion! And that is exactly the kind of leadership this world is going to need to usher in the Kingdom that is coming.

But sadly, instead of taking dominion in the world or the workplace, all too many believers relinquish their God-given right to dominion in the hopes of maybe witnessing to a few friends or co-workers on the way to the rapture. We too often see work (or everything else) as a necessary evil, something we do to get us by until Sunday, where the *real* work of the Kingdom supposedly occurs.

Let me give you an example of how many believers view workplace "dominion." Imagine you come home one day to

---

22   http://www.chick-fil-a.com/Company/Highlights-Sunday

find a pipe has burst and there is water filling your kitchen. You run to grab the Yellow Pages, quickly turn to the "Plumber" section, and call the first plumber you find. He has a Christian fish symbol next to his advertisement, so he's got to be good.

Fifteen minutes later, your plumber arrives. He takes a look at your kitchen and then proceeds to walk back to his truck, drop his tool belt, and grab his briefcase. To your utter shock and amazement, you then watch this plumber walk from door to door in your neighborhood. When he gets to the first house, he whips out an evangelistic tract so he can share Christ with your neighbor. He does this at the next house and then the next. This goes on for two hours. Finally, he returns to his truck, gets his belt, and fixes the pipe in twenty minutes. Then, he hands you a bill for three hours of work.

Let me ask you a simple question: would you be a little upset at this plumber?

Sure.

The real question is "why?" I mean, he was doing the "work of the Kingdom." He was, after all, sharing his faith—and there is nothing more important than that, right?

Wrong.

In that instance, the work of the Kingdom is to skillfully fix the leak—and all in the name of Christ. The job of the Christian worker is *first* excellence then witnessing. You can't witness effectively until you have done your job effectively—on time and on budget. I am sick and tired of Christian men and women being the worst workers on the job. The proverb is true:

"they are too 'spiritually-minded' to be of any earthly good." Their condemnation is just, and the world lies lost and in need of Christ.

What, then, is the purpose of all of this aggressive military action on behalf of the Kingdom? It's simple. God is going to give us ownership of all things, and he intends for us to start now. You are probably familiar with the Bible verse, "seek first the kingdom of God and his righteousness, and all these things will be added to you" (Matthew 6:33). It is often used as a way of excusing believers for not owning all spheres of life.

Well, do you want to know what Jesus said right after that? It's in Luke: "Fear not, little flock, for it is your Father's good pleasure *to give you the kingdom*" (Luke 12:32, emphasis mine). The tense is present—and I am pretty sure the Son of God knew how to conjugate verbs.

Christ is giving us the Kingdom, and so it's high time we went ahead and *got* the Kingdom.

The call for the Christian warrior is clear: we are to take dominion and redeem *all* areas of our society. Then, and only then, will the Kingdom finally come. So stop looking at the clouds, and stop listening to the ridiculous and never-ending predictions of the Second Coming. There is work to be done, and Christ's kingdom is on the move. You are the invasion force, and that invasion includes owning *everything*.

But before we take up arms, we must get very clear about our *mission*, and we must be precise about our *purpose*. And *that* we will cover in the next section.

SECTION 3:

CHRIST THE MAN ON A MISSION

SECTION 3:
CHRIST THE MAN ON A MISSION

"The intention of God is that we should each become the kind of person whom he can set free in his universe, empowered to do what we want to do. Just as we desire and intend this, so far as possible, for our children and others we love, so God desires and intends it for his children. But character, the inner directedness of the self, must develop to the point where that is possible."[23]

— Dallas Willard

"And He said to them, 'Why did you seek Me? Did you not know that I must be about My Father's business?'"

— Luke 2:49 NKJV

---

23   Willard, *The Divine Conspiracy*, 379.

A SCENE TOWARD THE end of the movie *Apollo 13* moves me to tears every time I watch it. The spacecraft has been in jeopardy for days, and it is time to bring it home. The valiant crew of Jim Lovell, Fred Haise, and Jack Swigert has done what they can. Now it's up to the parachute to do the rest.

Back on earth, the entire family and a host of friends gather at Marilyn Lovell's house. She's the wife of Apollo 13's commander.

Among the guests that night is Jim Lovell's mom, an elderly woman who Marilyn Lovell simply wants to keep distracted long enough to not worry about her boy. She brings over a few *noteworthy* guests to help sit with her mother-in-law.

Marilyn Lovell: Blanche, Blanche, these nice young men are going to watch the television with you. This is Neil Armstrong, and this is Buzz ... Aldrin.

Neil Armstrong: Hi.

Blanche Lovell: Are you boys in the space program too?[24]

The scene shifts back to the spacecraft and to the wearied men on board. Final preparations are being made for entry to earth's atmosphere. The cabin is prepared, a final rocket burn completed, and the astronauts strap in asking themselves the question: *having come so far, will the spacecraft make it safely through earth's atmosphere?*

Earlier, at the nursing home, young Susan Lovell approached her elderly grandmother. She had tears in her eyes and could barely get a word out. Unswayed, her grandmother took her by the hand, and as only a grandmother can she said,

Blanche Lovell: Are you scared?

Susan Lovell: [nods]

Blanche Lovell: Don't you worry. If they could get a washing machine to fly, my Jimmy could land it.[25]

It's enough to take your breath away.

You know the rest of the story. After what seems like hours, the pod is spotted, the men are alive, and what started as a disaster turns into one of NASA's finest hours.

The story, in its simplest form, is a tale about three men and a team of engineers who have all been perfectly called and equipped to accomplish a *mission.*

---

24   *Apollo 13,* directed by Ron Howard (Universal City, CA: Imagine Entertainment, 1995).

25   Ibid.

And what is true for the space program was doubly true for the Son of God. His mission was risky, perilous, and *absolutely necessary*. Jesus would not be deterred from his purpose, although hell and all the earth tried to sway him from it.

So as we travel into the gospel of Mark, the warrior theme is exactly that: Jesus, a Man on a Mission.

Mark slingshots Jesus onto the scene: "Now after John was arrested, Jesus came into Galilee, proclaiming the gospel of God, and saying, 'The time is fulfilled'" (Mark 1:14–15).

Jesus yelled, "Game on!" then, like a prizefighter, he came out of the corner swinging. In only a few short chapters of Mark, Jesus healed disease, cast out demons, calmed the storm, and by the end of chapter 3, a bounty was on his head. It seems people on a mission—at least this kind of mission—had no place in a Jewish kingdom ruled by the comfortable and callus.

In the beginning of Mark, we find a thoroughly disruptive story that offers a spot-free glance into the mission of the Servant King. Jesus set up a base around his hometown, Capernaum, a city on the northern shore of Galilee. It was a safe place, far enough from Jerusalem for him to train his disciples without bringing on too many death threats.

As Jesus got more popular, his ministry picked up a frenetic pace. In the morning he taught in the synagogue and cast out demons. That afternoon, he retired to Peter's house, presumably for some rest, but then the word got out: "That evening at sundown they brought to him all who were sick or oppressed by demons. *And the whole city was gathered together at the door.* And he healed many who were sick with various diseases, and cast out many demons. And he would not permit the demons to speak, because they knew him" (Mark 1:32–34, emphasis mine).

Imagine what it would be like to have the entire city gathered at *your* door. Picture a World War II hospital near Bastogne, France. Peter's overcrowded home probably smelled like a mix of gangrene, sweat, and urine, but then again what would you expect?

Some of the folks at the door were possessed by demons, others had a list of diseases a mile long, and many had been like that for a while. No one, Peter's mom included, had any idea when the line would slow down long enough for her to get the roast out of the oven and break out a game of Uno.

Chances are Jesus finished his work around 2:00 in the morning. Then he headed off to bed but not for long. According to the text, it sounds like he only got a few hours' sleep. That's because "Rising very early in the morning, while it was still dark, he departed and went out to a desolate place, and there he prayed" (Mark 1:35).

Jesus was tired, but then again that was all the more reason to get some time with his dad. Jesus took a risk in coming to this world as a man, and, needless to say, that risk was heightened when he did not get his alone time in prayer.[26]

---

26   As an aside, this passage is often used as a sort of a Christian guilt-trip. "If Jesus got up early to pray, so should you, you guilty sinner, you!" The point is not that Jesus got up to pray, nor that there was

So, here comes an interesting twist in the plot.

At this point in the book of Mark, Jesus' ministry had just taken off. He had a lot of new followers, and he had already proven he was the Man with a capital "M." He healed the sick, cast out demons, and spoke with a great deal of authority. In short, he was the one they had been waiting to see for quite a long time.

As popular as he was becoming, Jesus probably started to get a crowd of new folks around him for the purpose of giving him advice. Let's just say they are the first-century version of "ministry consultants." You can imagine them saying to themselves, "If he's going to lead us to victory over Rome, perhaps he could use some good people like us on his cabinet."

And then Jesus did something that shocked his self-appointed cabinet members into early retirement: "And Simon and those who were with him searched for him, and they found him and said to him, 'Everyone is looking for you.' And he said to them, 'Let us go on to the next town, that I may preach there also, for that is why I came out.' And he went throughout all Galilee, preaching in their synagogues and casting out demons" (Mark 1:36–39).

---

anything special about the early morning. The point was that he needed to be alone for a while, and he needed to pray, recharge, reconnect, and refresh. He was a man, after all, and every man needs some affirmation from his dad before launching into the mission of life—Jesus included. If the Son of God needed to connect with the heavenly Dad, so do you.

Can't you just see the jaws dropping in utter disbelief? Jesus had a crowd of people waiting for him in the square in front of the Capernaum Court House. Everyone was there. (Some translations say, "ALL men are looking for you.")

So what did Jesus do?

Actually, before you answer that, let me ask you a different question.

What would you do?

Your ministry has just kicked off and you have a crowd of people waiting on *your* every word. The sanctuary is packed, the microphone is on, and the band just finished the last verse of "Amazing Grace." Everyone is expecting you to show up and give a clever speech, heal the sick, and just be amazing.

In a characteristic twist of logic, given this very same situation, Jesus took a right hand turn and blew off the entire town.

It's staggering and I love him for this.

You see, in our day of e-mail, text, iPhone, Blackberry, Crackberry, instant noodles, instant coffee, instant message, instant gratification, and instant whatever-else-is-instant, we have literally lost the ability to say *no* to distraction and to stay on our mission. It's as though we now live totally on the defensive, beholden to every whim and desire of everyone who has a whim and a desire.

But not so for Jesus...

Christ was ultra-clear on exactly why he was placed on this earth—and tells Peter's mom, sorry for the crowd, but his mission wasn't to heal everyone in Capernaum.

Let's go to the next town to preach. That's why I came.

The ministry consultants blew their lid and marched off to find someone with a bit more, well, compassion. Jesus headed to the next town, and you know the rest. He did what he did as well as anyone has ever done it, and as a way of saying thanks for helping their people, the Jewish leaders issued another warrant for his arrest—and this time they meant it.

The warrior theme in the book of Mark is all about what it means to be a *man on a mission*. It describes Jesus as a person who went purposefully across the country looking to save the *right* people, not *all* people. It speaks of a man who knew what he was supposed to do and then did it. It tells of the Savior who battled storms and spirits to save only one man. And it describes a man who gave that same mission to his friends, a list of warriors that includes you and me.

CHAPTER 7:

DISCOVERING YOUR MISSION

IF JESUS WAS serious about his mission, we should be too. But then again, it is pretty difficult to hit a target you can't see.

When I was at the height of my career as an F-18 pilot, I was the leading instructor in the Marine Corps for aerial combat—one-against-one, plane-against-plane "dogfighting." You've probably seen the movie *Top Gun*, so you know what air combat is all about. During my time as an instructor, I taught our young Marine pilots some quite advanced tactics and maneuvers. The key to victory, however, was often simple.

Contrary to *Top Gun*, the most important rule of aerial fighting is not "never leave your wingman." The key to victory is:

When you lose sight, you lose the fight.

Read the history of the most famous dogfights of all time. In many cases, the successful aces had the ability to come out of the sun, to hide in the clouds, or to get the enemy to lose them all together. When the enemy can't see you, flying in air combat gets easy, so easy it's almost an unfair advantage.

Of course, on the flip side of this is the pilot's ability to stay focused on the enemy, to concentrate fully on the target.

And the same is true for your God-given mission. You can't hit a target you can't see.

And so the first step for being *on* mission is to *discover* what your mission is in the first place. That's means finding the enemy plane before he finds you. The second step is to *stay* on your mission. That's means keeping track of the enemy's plane until you shoot it down. Both discovering your mission and staying on your mission involve a fight.

Let's talk first about what it takes to discover your mission.

Start by answering this question: what did God place you on this earth to do? In other words, what is your mission in life? It is a question that deserves much thought, prayer, and council, but all too often, our search for true mission gets lost in the daily hustle and bustle of life.

Teaching you the details of finding your mission would take an entire book all by itself—and there are already many good books on the subject. So I will simply give you a few big-picture concepts and then refer you to the resources section at the back of the book.

First, accurately discovering your mission is nearly impossible if you are not walking conversationally, one-on-one with God. That's what Jesus did. He talked with the Father early in the morning—presumably to get his guidance and instruction for the day. Talking with God can be as natural as talking with a friend. Think about the people whom have been mentors in your life. What do all of those people have in common?

Answer: they spent a considerable amount of time talking with you. The same should be true with you and God. He is called the "Word," and it stands to reason he is called that because he has something to *say*. It also stands to reason he didn't stop talking back in AD 70, but that is another discussion for another day.

Just do it. *Try it*. Get alone and quiet with God and see what he has to say.[27]

27　I attended a four-day Christian men's retreat where the leaders purposefully set aside several hours each day for what they called "a covenant of silence." It was a time for the men to be quiet and listen to God. For me, the time was glorious. Without the distractions of everyday life, I was able to communicate with God on a very close level. On the afternoon of the third day (and in the middle of an hour-long covenant of silence), I retreated to my dorm room to pick up some supplies. What I found there was heartbreaking: four men engaged in a theological debate as to whether God still speaks. It was a perfect analogy for the church today. Instead of listening to God, we drown out his voice with debates as to whether or not he speaks at all. To be sure, debate is far more comfortable than communion with God but far less effective.

This is very important. God speaks to us in multiple ways through multiple means. He speaks through others, he speaks through his still small voice, and he speaks through nature. But the *primary* way in which God speaks is through his Word. I am consistently amazed at how applicable the written Word of God is for every situation of life. And therefore, it must be the very basis for everything else we hear, see, or feel. If anything we hear contradicts God's written Word, we reject it, no matter how compelling. If anything agrees with God's written Word, we receive it, no matter how much it contradicts our apparent life situation.

Another key component to discovering your true mission is to find out what you *like to do*. Desire is the key to your heart's calling. Given the opportunity, your good heart will guide you to your good calling.[28] That's because God has already written that desire on your heart in the first place.

In the *Awakened Heart*, Gerald May puts it this way: "It is possible to run away from the desire for years, even for decades, at a time, but we cannot eradicate it entirely. It keeps touching us in little hints in our dreams, our hopes, our unguarded moments....It is who we are."[29]

Speaking of the heart as the key to mission, John Eldredge says,

---

28   I am indebted to both Gary Barkalow and John Eldredge for helping me understand that my heart was the key to my calling. See the resources from both of them at the end of the book.

29   Gerald May, *The Awakened Heart* (New York, NY: Harper Collins, 1993), 3.

This may come as a surprise to you: Christianity is not an invitation to become a moral person. It is not a program for getting us in line or for reforming society. It has a powerful effect upon our lives, but when transformation comes, it is always the after effect of something else, something at the level of our hearts. At its core, Christianity begins with an invitation to desire. Look again at the way Jesus relates to people. As he did with the fellow at the Sheep Gate, he is continually taking them into their hearts, to their deepest desires.[30]

Tragically, one of the places where this idea of mission quickly dies is in the church. It should be the other way around, but all too often the prevailing goal of the church is the church's *program* and the prevailing spirit is *guilt*. In all too many churches, the most important thing you can do is volunteer your time for the latest and greatest program. If you don't, well, just wait until next Sunday's sermon; you'll get another chance.

I have a fundamental belief that the large majority of real Christian service is actually supposed to occur *outside* the walls of church, meaning at home, at work, on the streets, and in everyday conversation. Heck, that's how Jesus did it. Sure, ministry occurs at church too. And that's why I also believe God, in his providence, has strategically placed all the gifts necessary in each whole church for that church to thrive. When Jesus said the church was his body, he meant it. And it's hard to

---

30   John Eldredge, *Desire* (Nashville, TN: Thomas Nelson, 2007), 35.

imagine Jesus' body missing a bunch of parts. So, for example, I believe in every whole church, people are right there to do the necessary work. But sadly, more often than not, all the "body" parts end up in the wrong places.

Lori has the gift of music, and God put her there to lead the choir. But Jane has been doing it for years, and she's not budging. So Mary ends up in the children's ministry. It's not that she doesn't like kids; she just longs for something more.

John has a teacher's heart. He loves to share God's Word in new and inspiring ways. The leaders of the church however are quite happy with the teaching team they have in place. It's more comfortable the way it is. And John, well, John seems a bit too confident. They call that pride and keep him in his place. So John ends up leading the local Rotary Club.

Fred and Charity have the gift of hospitality. They thrive on sharing their home as a refuge for the lost, the outcast, and the disillusioned. But the church wants them working *inside* the walls. So instead of having the time to serve at home, they end up leading the Sunday morning snack program.

Tony is a master at sales—what he does in the workplace is simply stunning. And when he does it well, he gives great glory to God by valiantly creating massive revenue streams. But the church doesn't recognize selling as "kingdom work." Instead of affirming and further equipping Tony, he ends up leading the evangelism study group on Tuesday nights.

The examples are endless.

If we only used the time to ask God where he would have us, then we could proceed without all the guilt to becoming a whole and holy church that would really get things done for the Kingdom.

Let me say this as clearly as I can: if you are doing something in your church and the primary reason you are doing it is because you would feel guilty for saying no, you are doing the *wrong* thing in your church. Go and find out what you do really well, what you want to do, and then go do *that* for the Kingdom.

Several years ago I visited a church and was treated to twenty-five minutes of the best sermon I had heard in a long time. The pastor waxed eloquently about the need for selfless people to rise up and serve Christ. I could not have been more engaged. Had he just stopped there, led us in a verse of "Onward Christian Soldier," and served communion, we all would have been better for having been there.

The problem was his sermon had five more minutes left. Like a pin popping a balloon at a rest home, the pastor transitioned into his main "application" point, "And that's why I want you to strongly consider serving this church and using your talents right here. The parking ministry needs people, and you could certainly use some of your time on Sunday to help our guests find a spot."

(sigh)

Good news: the Toyotas and Buicks are parked in neat little rows outside of the community church.

Bad news: an expectant world lies dying and in need of Christ.

It would be comical if it weren't so true. You can almost hear the enemy laughing. "Let's get them all excited about the latest program. That will keep them busily distracted from doing *anything* worth doing."

Bill Johnson, the pastor of Bethel Church in Redding, California, puts it this way: "There is no such thing as secular employment for the believer. Once we are born again, everything about us is redeemed for Kingdom purposes. It is all spiritual. It is either legitimate Kingdom expression, or we shouldn't be involved at all."[31]

All I can say is this. If you have come this far in this little book, there is hope. Indeed, there is great hope for you. My guess is the last few paragraphs may have stirred up in you a longing for something more, something better, something far more impactful than parking cars (however noble that may be).

If so, fan that flame, my friend. Fan it long and fan it strong. Walk with God and ask him your deepest questions. Listen, you do not have to be afraid of coming to his throne. You don't need a week of fasting and perfect obedience to get an audience with the King. If you have come to Christ, your sin has been covered and God thinks you are pretty cool. And about all of that condemnation and guilt you are feeling right now; that's not from Him. The devil is the one called the accuser. The Holy Spirit, well, he is the Comforter. If you're feeling accused and Christ has forgiven you, then it's not Christ accusing you.

---

31   Bill Johnson, *Dreaming with God* (Shippensburg, PA: Destiny Image, 2006), 89.

My friend Steve Brown says, "By far, the most salient reason we don't pray much is our guilt."[32] So get past all that guilt and get with your Father.

Let me say this as clearly as I can. While my focus in the book has primarily been on Christ as your example, your first step must always be to receive him as your *substitute*. His death, resurrection, and ascension are the only things that bring you into true holiness and humanity. That's why your first move as a warrior is the most contradictory one of all: you surrender. You bow the knee to your Captain and ask him to give you what you could never get by yourself. There is no special formula for this, nor is there a special prayer. You simply admit you are weak, he is strong, and you need him to save you from *everything*.

Much like the daddy of the prodigal son, when you come home to your Father, you will find open arms, a strong hug, and a splendid dinner with wine, dancing, and more wine.

So, go to him and ask him to accept you as his son. Then, ask him about your mission and purpose in life. Finally, start asking others. Ask your pastor. Ask your friends. Ask them what one thing you could do to make a big difference in the world today.

Then, when you find that one thing...well, do it.

Now, before I leave the issue of calling, let me say this. You may already be doing what you are called to do. If that's the case, great! In fact, if you look close, you will always find

---

32   Steve Brown, *Three Free Sins* (Brentwood, TN: Howard Books, 2012), 144.

callings that have already been assigned to you. So, you might as well get good at it. For example, moms and dads are called to be great moms and dads. Husbands and wives are called to be great husbands and wives. And as for the job you're doing now, well, the Bible says you ought to be doing that with all of your might (Colossians 3:23).

Far too often, we believe "true Christian service" is found only in those activities that seem sanctified, spiritualized, and oh so holy. But more times than not, your mission may be found in the truly secular: industry, art, science, parenting, and even sales. Are you skilled in one of these areas or perhaps another, "non-churchy" gift? If so, it is quite likely God is calling you to do just that—and to do it well.

I was once very good at dropping bombs from a plane moving at high rates of speed. At the top of my career as a Marine F-18 pilot, I could drop a 1,000-pound bomb eight miles away and nail the target within seven meters or less. That, my friend, takes skill. And that "calling" (believe it or not) is just as "holy" as preaching, witnessing, or leading the choir.

Agnes Sanford puts it this way:

And never forget that God is a maker, a doer, a worker—a Creator! His creativity functions on every plane, not merely on that plane that we are pleased to call "spiritual." If there were no bridge-builders in the world and no auto mechanics, no schoolteachers, and no inventors, the world that God is building through man upon this planet would fall to pieces. If, on the other hand, we would all seek God's gift of wisdom in whatever we do, we would create an efficiency, an integrity, a vision, greater than anything we have seen, and God's Kingdom of Heaven would have a material framework in which to grow.[33]

Do you want to know what God wants you to do with your life? Ask diligently and seek with all of your heart. Perhaps God has something planned, a new way to use your gifts. Perhaps it is a new or expanded application of what you currently do you would know nothing about until you ask him.

Finding your mission takes time, patience, and walking with God. But calling is essential to living as a warrior for Christ. And once you get clear on your target, it becomes that much easier to hit it.

---

33 Agnes Sanford, *The Healing Gifts of the Spirit* (New York, NY: Harper Collins, 1984), 83.

CHAPTER 8:

STAYING ON
YOUR MISSION

NOW, AND THIS is important, once you find your mission, it is imperative then to *stay* on your mission. This also involves a fight.

I have flown close to 2,000 hours in the FA-18 Hornet fighter jet. From experience, I can tell you the plane is truly one of the most remarkable engineering feats known to man. The Hornet can fly up to 50,000 feet above the ground and up to two times the speed of sound (around 1,200 miles per hour). But then again, many fighter airplanes can do that. What made the Hornet so different is the fact it's the first airplane able to shoot *both* air-to-air missiles and air-to-ground bombs. FA-18 pilots can fight their way through enemy fighters, destroy the target, then fight their way home.

Before the Hornet, there were "bomber" airplanes and "fighter" airplanes. And, in almost every case, the bombers needed a fighter escort. Not so anymore.

With all the complicated systems and missions, we FA-18 pilots train every day to focus on the specific mission at hand. Fighting airplanes requires a totally different skill set than dropping bombs. And both require serious concentration. So, pilots learn quite early on the importance of *focus*, staying on mission. If a pilot is thinking about dropping bombs while fighting an enemy airplane, he will die. That alone is sufficient motivation indeed.

Sadly, staying on mission in the Christian life is not so clear cut. To be sure, it is still a war and there are still casualties. It's just hard to see through the daily clutter long enough to focus on the larger battles. But then again, Christ was not immune to the temptation to get off mission. Let's look at one such time.

A passage right at the end of Mark 3 is so confusing, so disturbing, we literally read right past it without stopping to ask why Jesus did what he did. It came during one of those times of teaching, healing, and deliverance.

> And his mother and his brothers came, and standing outside they sent to him and called him. And a crowd was sitting around him, and they said to him, "Your mother and your brothers are

outside, seeking you." And he answered them, "Who are my mother and my brothers?" And looking about at those who sat around him, he said, "Here are my mother and my brothers! For whoever does the will of God, he is my brother and sister and mother." (Mark 3:31–35)

Now be perfectly honest. Doesn't Jesus' reaction sound a bit harsh? In the Jewish culture, much like ours, family was *everything*. This was the Virgin Mary —the same one who spoke to the angel Gabriel, met the wise men, and ran away to Egypt to save baby Messiah's life. Jesus could have at least let her into the house. I mean, it was his mom, for heaven's sake. The fifth commandment clearly states that we honor our father and mother. That little stunt of his doesn't sound like honor, does it? Didn't she deserve a *little* respect?

Apparently not.

Jesus blew off his mom...in front of everyone! Can you believe that? Mary was literally left standing in the heat and dust outside while Jesus sat comfortably on the couch teaching. It seems so...*un-Christlike*.

That is until you know the rest of the story. You see, taken out of context, Jesus' reaction was just plain mean—and he's left without any excuse for his lack of courtesy. Then again, everything Jesus did was motivated by love. So let's see what was really occurring there.

Earlier in the chapter, Mark tells us why Jesus' mom was really in town that day: "Then he went home, and the crowd gathered again, so that they could not even eat. And when his family heard it, they went out to seize him, for they were saying, 'He is out of his mind'" (Mark 3:20–21).

Ah, now it's starting to make sense. Mary and the boys were coming to town for one reason: Jesus needed to be stopped. They knew he was special, but in all honesty, they thought he was taking this whole mission thing a bit too far. They were certain he had lost his mind, and they were coming to tell him so.

Now, imagine what would have happened had Jesus let his mom in the house that day. In front of a crowd of about fifty people, Mary would have publically told Jesus something like this: "Son, you are out of your mind. Stop all this teaching, healing, and demon rebuking. It's ridiculous. Who do you think you are? Take my hand, son, you need help. Come home this very instant!"

Given this scenario, Christ would have been forced to rebuke his mother in plain daylight. She would have been shocked, embarrassed, and nothing would have been the same ever again, for Jesus or for Mary. Jesus instead showed his mom untold compassion. He likely saved his rebuke for a quieter moment none of the gospel writers ever witnessed. In short, he *rescued* Mary's reputation by blowing her off.

It was kindness in action.

Christ was so focused, so determined on accomplishing his mission, that no one, not even his family members could steer him away from it. When you think about this from the enemy's perspective, it was quite a clever ploy. If anyone could sway Jesus, even for a while, it would have been his mom. But

Christ didn't take the bait. He so cleverly reversed the situation that his family would sit in the shadows for years to come.

The point is obvious. First, when God calls you to accomplish a mission, that is exactly what you do, despite all the evidence to the contrary. Your friends, family, even your spouse may not like it, but then again, you report to your Commander and him alone. This, of course, does not preclude the need for wise council. Many men have done things in the name of Christ they were never called to do—and they lost their families as a result. Don't be one of them.

But on the flip side, following Jesus on mission sometimes involves doing things that seem a bit extreme. And the ever-present temptation is to back off, slow down, or just abandon the mission all together. Listen, this is important, if your mission is truly God-given, it will be difficult and it will be opposed. Expect that. The victory on the other side is worth it, and that fact alone is enough reason to stay focused, come what may.

I'll be honest, for much of my life, my unstated life mission was to simply live a happy life and be comfortable. That didn't cut it and frankly I hated it. And so did God.

Now I have a passion for stamping out unbelief inside and outside the church. It took a great deal of inner-healing and communion with God to get clear on that mission, but now that I have found it, oh brother, what I wouldn't do to *stay* on it.

All by itself, staying on mission takes fighting, especially when it comes to managing your limited time. So, let me give you a very practical example of what I mean by staying on my mission.

Right now, my mission is to write this book. Most authors take a year (or more) to get a book done. I am currently on day 2. Just about every word you have read so far has been written in the last forty-eight hours and mostly between the hours of 10 a.m. and 5 p.m. How was I able to do that? Well, for one, I have up until this point checked my email a grand total of two times and for a grand total of about twenty minutes. The first thing I did for the last two days when I walked into my office was to write, and usually for several hours. That is what I call "taking the offensive." What do most people do when they first arrive at the office? Check email. And that's what I call "being on the defensive."

Additionally, staying on this mission has been a battle like I have never seen before. Finances were tight, tempers flared, and the first draft read like a kindergarten paper. But through it all, God has sustained me with a quiet confidence that this mission is *worth it*. It was hard—very hard—but then again, when you do what God wants you to do, it is sure to be difficult for a while. After a while, God shows up, the fog lifts, and the enemy flees.

Staying on mission involves saying no—a lot. As you begin to execute the mission God has called you to do, people will take notice. When they do, they are going to start asking you to participate in their pet missions and programs. It's natural. They want help—and they know you are a person who can get a job done. But if what they are asking you to do is not in line with your calling and God doesn't have that for you, it's not your job. Period. So, if someone (no matter how influential they are) asks you to take on a mission you are not called to, you have a moral obligation to say no.

You don't need to apologize, and you don't need a long list of excuses. Just say no. Far too many Christians live their entire lives in a frenetic rush from one distraction to another. And all the while, the world waits desperately for your gifts to heal their land.

Richard Foster puts it this way: "In contemporary society our Adversary majors in three things: noise, hurry, and crowds. If he can keep us engaged in 'much-ness' and 'many-ness' he will rest satisfied."[34]

This, of course, is not an excuse for selfishness. Diapers need changing, dishes need washing, floors need cleaning, and the trash needs to be taken out. Mission should never be a veiled excuse for laziness. Try that one at home, "Sorry, honey, I can't put the kids to bed (ever). I need to stay on mission, and right now God is calling me to watch Monday Night Football."

Many times our mission really means accomplishing multiple "assignments" near-simultaneously. So, just use your best wisdom and walk with God.

To summarize, being a person on a mission involves two things: discovering it and then doing it. First, you need to

---

34   Richard Foster, *The Celebration of Discipline* (New York, NY: Harper Collins, 1988), 15.

get clear on the mission God has put you on this planet to accomplish. Most Christians aren't, but that doesn't mean you need to have some kind of a guilt trip about it. Then, once you're clear on mission, take the helm and steer your ship in the direction he intends you to steer, without distractions.

CHAPTER 9:
MISSION TAKES RISK

O N JUNE 5, 1944, the day before D-Day, Dwight D. Eisenhower sat alone in his makeshift field office. He had just finalized the order to send 156,000 troops and 11,590 aircraft across the British Channel and into the teeth of the German defenses at Normandy. He also sent an inspiring letter to the troops:

> Soldiers, Sailors and Airmen of the Allied Expeditionary Force!
>
> You are about to embark upon the Great Crusade, toward which we have striven these many months. The eyes of the world are upon you. The hopes

and prayers of liberty-loving people everywhere march with you. In company with our brave Allies and brothers-in-arms on other Fronts, you will bring about the destruction of the German war machine, the elimination of Nazi tyranny over the oppressed peoples of Europe, and security for ourselves in a free world.

Your task will not be an easy one. Your enemy is well trained, well equipped and battle hardened. He will fight savagely.

But this is the year 1944! Much has happened since the Nazi triumphs of 1940-1941. The United Nations have inflicted upon the Germans great defeats, in open battle, man-to-man. Our air offensive has seriously reduced their strength in the air and their capacity to wage overwhelming superiority in weapons and munitions of war, and placed at our disposal great reserves of trained fighting men. The tide has turned! The free men of the world are marching together to Victory! I have full confidence in your courage, devotion to duty and skill in battle. We will accept nothing less than full Victory!

Good Luck! And let us beseech the blessing of Almighty God upon this great and noble undertaking.

Signed....Dwight D. Eisenhower[35]

---

35   http://www.ddaymuseum.co.uk/d-day/d-day-and-the-battle-of-normandy-your-questions-answered   and   http://www.american-presidents.org/2009/06/eisenhowers-d-day-letter.html

What you might not know is that very same day, Eisenhower wrote a second (and altogether different) letter. This one was written to the American people. The letter was never published because it never *needed* to be published.

> Our landings in the Cherbourg-Havre area have failed to gain a satisfactory foothold and I have withdrawn the troops. My decision to attack at this time and place was based upon the best information available. The troop, the air [force] and the navy did all that bravery and devotion to duty could do. If any blame or fault attaches to the attempt, it is mine alone.[36]

It is hard to grasp the gravity of the situation. That's because reading back into history, we know D-Day was a huge success. We struck at the right time; we struck at the right place; and Eisenhower would eventually win the war, liberate France, and become the thirty-fourth president of the United States.

We have the luxury of knowing how the story turned out.

But on the night of June 5, 1944, Eisenhower sat in his study, without a clue as to how many men he had just sent to their deaths. He had no idea if the attack would succeed or whether it would be a failed attempt to gain a foothold in France. And so he courageously wrote the most poignant letter of his life—one acknowledging all the risk—and taking all the blame.

---

36   David Howarth, *Dawn of D-Day: These Men Were There* (New York, NY: Skyhorse Publishing, 2008), 32.

The point is simple: war means taking risks.

So much more than the Normandy invasion, sending Christ to Earth took an enormous risk.[37] Christ had only one option: he had to prevail. He had to be victorious. Never was more at stake. Never did more lives hang in the balance. The future of the entire world, the entire creation, waited for this very moment. That's because, on the night Jesus was born, the God of the universe, the Son of God, emptied himself of his forever-past glory and became a...man.

Over the next thirty-three years, Jesus encountered wave after wave of struggle, thirst, hunger, fatigue, and temptation beyond anything any of us could stand.

Just imagine living a life where one sin (no matter how small) would bring an end to the world as we know it. It's almost impossible to fathom.

---

37   The concept of God taking risks is indeed a touchy, debated issue. The question comes down to the mystery of Christ's humanity (depths that we will never be able to completely plumb). Jesus was in fact God, and God knows everything and controls everything. But Jesus was also all man. And so because of that mystery, I am willing to tread lightly here. In other words, the idea of God taking risks is not a hill on which I am willing to die. Many men take an opposing viewpoint on the issue, and I respect them for it. One such man is John Piper. His opposing viewpoint can be found in his book *The Pleasures of God* (pp. 55-62). Piper is a much better theologian than I am, so if you are on the fence here, go with Piper. But wherever you land, it is still true that we are called to take risks and that Christ fiercely battled sin (which had to be possible for temptation to be temptation). That is my main point anyway, so don't lose that amidst the theological debate that is shrouded in a mystery we may never figure out.

One slip up, one glance too long, one vile thought, just one short fantasy, two more glasses of wine, one angry outburst (it would have felt so good), one misplaced word, one failure. Just one—*just one* and everything falls apart.

Imagine, perhaps, the Godhead splits in two and who knows what kind of hell happens then. Surely, at the very least, all of creation falls to pieces. Christ, after all, holds the world together "by the word of his power" (Hebrews 1:3). We the people and soon-to-be people are cast into hell to suffer an eternity of pain, loss, and suffering. The clock stops ticking. The hosts of heaven stand breathless and defeated. God the Father withdraws to feel the deep loss of his Son for all eternity.

Heaven weeps.

Everything (and I mean everything) was riding on the success of that *one* man.

Can you imagine what life would be like to live for thirty-three years knowing you could not make *one* mistake?

It's breathtaking in its courageous magnitude.

Look at it this way. Adam had the entire garden to himself. He was perfectly sinless and lived in a perfectly sinless world. Even if he wanted to be angry, there wasn't even anything there to make Adam angry! Sexual temptation wasn't even a concept, much less a struggle. Coveting was nonexistent—he had everything he could ever want.

Adam had one single, teeny-weenie command: don't eat from the fruit of that one tree.

A few days into Paradise, Adam and Eve had a fruit salad and the rest is history.

Four thousand years later, Christ was born into a world not with one command but with pages and pages of commandments (with case laws to reinforce them). He was born into a fallen world, deep in sin, and readily providing every temptation imaginable.

Adam fell when it was easy.

Christ prevailed when it was *difficult*.

The point is crystal clear. If you are going to become a warrior like Christ, you must know fighting in this war takes on immense risk. The amazing news is God, he who leads you, was not afraid of risk-taking.

Recently, I was talking with a friend about how valiantly Christ endured the temptation in the wilderness. Jesus was tired, hungry, and thirsty. He was surrounded by wild animals, and yet, even while facing the Prince of Darkness himself, Christ prevailed. He didn't just scrape by either; he slam-dunked Satan into next week.

As I was remarking about how hard it must have been to resist this kind of temptation, my friend looked at me and said, "Yeah, but that was Christ. He was God after all." She totally dismissed the power of that temptation based on the fact Jesus was God.

But the problem is you can't go there when it comes to his temptation and his humanity. For Christ to become a perfect sacrifice and to become a faithful High Priest, he had to have been temped as we are, in *all* things: "For we do not have a high priest who cannot sympathize with our weaknesses, but One who has been tempted *in all things as we are*, yet without sin" (Hebrews 4:15 NASB, emphasis mine).

Now I know a lot of people don't like the idea that God could have sinned, but it had to be that way (whether you like it or not.) In fact, it had to be that way whether you *understand* it or not. For temptation to be temptation, Jesus had to be able to sin. Of course, he did not sin, which makes his victory that much more amazing.

There are times when, to be blunt, we rest too much on the Deity of Christ, his being God. His temptation is one of those times. Let me give you an example. Can you picture Christ battling with sexual temptation? (Notice I said "temptation" and not "sin"). He was a single man. He must have been lonely. Do you think the devil used that fact to tempt him sexually? Of course! And if your view of Christ's humanity does not allow for him to be tempted in this way, yet without sin, your view of Christ's humanity is wrong.

Or what about Jesus' childhood? What is your concept of that? Does your mind automatically go to "Jesus, meek and mild," perfect and pure, never a care in the world, like a little round cherub, and adorned with a cute halo? I have news for you; Jesus threw up breast milk on Mary's shoulder just like you did on your mom's shoulder. He probably did it a few times. He was a man, just like you and me.

John Eldredge put it this way:

For ages upon ages, his generous hand fed every creature on earth; now it is he that has to be fed, spoon-fed, drooling most of it down his chin like any other toddler. The Son of God doesn't even know how to tie his shoes. Someone had to teach him how to tie those sandals John the Baptist said none of us were worthy to untie. "The rabbit goes around the tree and down through the hole...like that. Now you try it." Picture seven-year-old Jesus in the shop out back, learning from Joseph how to use a hammer and a saw. He who hung galaxies in such perfect poise, like a hundred billion mobiles, has to be shown how to nail two boards together.

I take my shoes off. The humility of this is beyond words.

Remember—Jesus wasn't faking it when he took on his humanity.[38]

And because he "wasn't faking it" he faced temptation and trial exactly like we face temptation and trial. And yet, unlike us, he did all that without sin. It's enough to take your breath away.

And so let's get back to the issue of risk. If God is a God who would risk it all to save his people—and if we are made in his image—then it stands to reason he made us people with a great capacity for risk. And it also stands to reason if you are not actively taking risks for the Kingdom, then you're missing out on a lot God has to offer.

---

38   John Eldredge, *Beautiful Outlaw* (Brentwood, TN: FaithWords, 2011), 109.

For example, if life has become a bit stale and you're feeling purposeless right now, perhaps you haven't risked much lately, or perhaps you haven't risked *at all*. You have a nice four-bedroom, two-and-a-half-bath house in the 'burbs, two cars, one point nine kids, and a comfy 401K. You're supposed to be happy, you are supposed to *feel* happy, but that only seems to come late at night after a few glasses of wine and reruns of *The Deadliest Catch*.

Then one day, you look up to realize everything you thought would bring you life is actually *killing you* with boredom.

So if I may be so bold, I would like to ask you this simple question:

What is God asking you to risk?

Perhaps it's your security, your finances, or your future. Perhaps it is your grasping and grabbing at life and not trusting in him to provide. Perhaps it's your time and the choice to use more of it for his kingdom, come what may.

Whatever it is, you can trust in one thing. When you take a risk to accomplish the mission God is asking you to execute, He comes through.

Listen: he always comes through. He *always* does.

The opposite of risk-taking and trusting in God's hand is safe, comfortable, and, oh, so faithless. "This is, in fact, how many professing Christians end up living as: practical agnostics. *Perhaps God will come through, perhaps he won't, so I'll be hanged if I'll live as though he had to come through. I'll hedge my bets and if he does show up, so much the better.* The simple word for this is godlessness."[39]

Now let me be very clear here: I am not telling you to shut down a business, quit your job, sell your house, and move to Zimbabwe just so you can take a risk. Nor am I saying risk-taking for risk-taking's sake is any better. As with anything, there is always the need for wisdom and council. Talk to God, and be sure you know what he wants you to do. Get good advice from men who have walked with you and know your strengths. Risk taking is hard enough. It's much harder still when you're blindly heading in a direction God has not called you to.

Of course, once you've figured out what, exactly, God is asking you to risk, there is basically one move left for you on the chessboard.

You do it. Period.

"Throughout Scripture we see that when God's people step forward to serve, God backs it up with power."[40]

Your personal Normandy invasion is on the horizon—and the spoils of victory are great. So, will you come and join the mighty few who are willing to take a risk for the King and accomplish your mission?

---

39   Brent Curtis and John Eldredge, *The Sacred Romance* (Nashville, TN: Thomas Nelson, 1997), 69.

40   Johnson, *Dreaming with God*, 97.

CHAPTER 10:
SOMETIMES THE MISSION IS A MAN

A SCENE A FEW chapters into Mark gives us a great insight into the heart of Christ for his people. The mission started with a storm:

On that day, when evening had come, he said to them, "Let us go across to the other side." And leaving the crowd, they took him with them in the boat, just as he was. And other boats were with him. And a great windstorm arose, and the waves were breaking into the boat, so that the boat was already filling. But he was in the stern, asleep on the cushion. And they woke him and said to him,

"Teacher, do you not care that we are perishing?"
And he awoke and rebuked the wind and said to
the sea, "Peace! Be still!" And the wind ceased, and
there was a great calm. He said to them, "Why are
you so afraid? Have you still no faith?" And they
were filled with great fear and said to one another,
"Who then is this, that even the wind and the sea
obey him?" (Mark 4:35–41)

Jesus was, in a word, tired. He hit the cushion at the back
of the boat and collapsed. He was the Son of Man, the Son of
God even, and he was taking a nap. His disciples, still struggling
with who they had in the boat, started to panic when the wind
howled and the waves roared. Between us, I don't think they
woke Jesus up so he would calm the storm. Just look at how
terrified they were once he *did* calm the storm. My guess is they
woke him up so he could share their common misery—just like
you do when your spouse is sound asleep and you are hearing
bumps in the night.

So, naturally, the boys woke Jesus up. He promptly rubbed
the sleep out of his eyes, stretched his arms, and calmed the sea.
Presumably, he then went back to the cushion and fell asleep
muttering "O, ye of little faith," or something like that, under
his breath.

But the story does not stop there. Let's pick it up in
Mark 5. This is where the real action begins:

They came to the other side of the sea, to the
country of the Gerasenes. And when Jesus had
stepped out of the boat, immediately there met
him out of the tombs a man with an unclean

spirit. He lived among the tombs. And no one could bind him anymore, not even with a chain, for he had often been bound with shackles and chains, but he wrenched the chains apart, and he broke the shackles in pieces. No one had the strength to subdue him. Night and day among the tombs and on the mountains he was always crying out and cutting himself with stones. And when he saw Jesus from afar, he ran and fell down before him. And crying out with a loud voice, he said, "What have you to do with me, Jesus, Son of the Most High God? I adjure you by God, do not torment me." For he was saying to him, "Come out of the man, you unclean spirit!" And Jesus asked him, "What is your name?" He replied, "My name is Legion, for we are many." And he begged him earnestly not to send them out of the country. Now a great herd of pigs was feeding there on the hillside, and they begged him, saying, "Send us to the pigs; let us enter them." So he gave them permission. And the unclean spirits came out, and entered the pigs, and the herd, numbering about two thousand, rushed down the steep bank into the sea and were drowned in the sea. (Mark 5:1–13)

Let's start by looking at the demonic host oppressing this man. This was far from a petty little band of impudent imps. A literal army of fallen warriors demonized this man. The head demon called his troops a "Legion." A Roman legion had as many as 6,000 troops.[41] Perhaps the demon leader was exaggerating his numbers. Either way, we know at least this: he represented at least 2,000 demons. That is the rough number of pigs that rushed into the sea when "Legion" was cast out.

Let's put this into context. It took two angels to decimate Sodom and Gomorrah. It took just one angel to wipe out every firstborn child in Egypt. In Revelation, only a few angels destroy a third of the earth's population. These are powerful creatures, and the fallen ones are just as powerful, inasmuch as they are evil. One demon is enough to make your life a living hell—how much more when you have 2,000 demons. Twelve young bucks from town tried all afternoon to wrap this guy up, and he kept breaking the chains. "No one had the strength to subdue him."

The Son of God stepped onto the shore at Gerasenes like an invasion force landing at Normandy. This was an all-out war—and Jesus was one against 2,000. Unlike the locals, Christ didn't have chains, clubs, spears, or any other physical weapons. He didn't need them. The demons were scared out of their minds, which may be why they tried opposing Christ the night before with a storm.[42] With nothing but his own word, Jesus

---

41   http://en.wikipedia.org/wiki/Roman_legion

42   The idea of demonic forces manipulating the weather is not a new biblical concept. In the book of Job, God allowed Satan to destroy everything that Job owned: "And the LORD said to Satan, 'Behold, all that he has is in your hand. Only against him do not stretch out your hand.' So Satan went out from the presence of the LORD.... and behold, a great wind came across the wilderness and struck the four corners of the house, and it fell upon the young people, and they are dead, and I alone have escaped to tell you" (Job 1:12, 19). This concept brings new light into the story of the evening storm

swept the power of hell and death out of this man; and the next thing we know, he was sitting on the shore having a little chat over a fish taco.

Now that's what you call *power*. The interesting thing is Jesus gives us every indication the same power is available to you and me. We just need to be on the right mission and tap into the right source. That power, incidentally, comes from three things, which we will cover in the next section.

Just think about this. Jesus Christ, the Son of God, battled sleep, battled discomfort, battled weather, and battled 2,000 demons to save *one* man. The text is very clear. When Jesus finished talking to the formerly demon-possessed man, he got right back into the boat and headed across the sea.

He spent one night and one day of his short, three-year ministry to save *one* man.

And he would do the same for *you*. In fact, he does it every single day.

Brennan Manning tells a similar story of love and redemption:

> Since moving to New Orleans, I've gotten deeply involved in the only leper colony in the United Sates. It's found in Carville, Louisiana, about twenty miles southwest of Baton Rouge. I've been there many, many times. I go from room to room visiting the lepers, victims of Hansen's disease.

that Jesus calmed...and it may also bring new light into the power of warfare prayer over the weather. Just food for thought.

On one occasion, as I was coming up the front steps, a nurse came running toward me and said, "Brennan, can you come quick and pray with Yolanda? She's dying, Brennan."

...I went up to Yolanda's room on the second floor and sat on the edge of the bed. Yolanda is a woman thirty-seven years old. Five years ago, before the leprosy began to ravage, she must have been one of the most stunningly beautiful creatures God ever made. I do not mean just a cute, pretty, or even attractive woman. I mean the kind of blinding physical beauty that causes men and women on the street to stop and stare. In pictures, Yolanda had the largest, most mesmerizing, most translucent brown eyes I've ever seen, set in the exquisitely chiseled face with high cheekbones, long brown hair down to a slender waist, and a perfectly proportioned bust. But that was then.

Now her nose is pressed into her face. Her mouth is severely contorted. Both ears are distended. She has no fingers on either hand, just two little stumps. One of the first effects of leprosy is losing all sensitivity in your extremities, toes and fingers. A leper can rest her hand on a burning hot stove and feel absolutely nothing; this often leads to gangrene and eventually demands amputation. Yolanda just had these two little stumps.

Two years earlier, her husband divorced her because of the social stigma attached to leprosy, and he had forbidden their two sons, boys fourteen and sixteen, from ever visiting their mother. The father was an alcoholic, complete with frequent violent mood swings. The boys were terrified of him, so they dutifully obeyed; as a result, Yolanda was dying an abandoned, forsaken woman.

I...prayed with her [Yolanda]. As I turned around... the room was filled with a brilliant light. It had been raining when I came in; I didn't even look up, but said, "Thanks, Abba, for the sunshine. I bet that'll cheer her up."

As I turned to look back at Yolanda—and if I live to be three hundred years old I'll never be able to find the words to describe what I saw—her face was like a sunburst over the mountains, like one thousand sunbeams streaming out of her face literally so brilliant I had to shield my eyes.

I said, "Yolanda, you appear to be very happy."

With her slight Mexican-American accent she said, "Oh, Father, I am so happy."

I then asked her, "Will you tell me why you're so happy?"

She said, "Yes, the Abba of Jesus just told me that He would take me home today."

I vividly remember the hot tears that began rolling down my cheeks. After a lengthy pause, I asked just what the Abba of Jesus said.

Yolanda said:

"Come now, My love. My lovely one, come.

For you, the winter has passed, the snows are over and gone, the flowers appear in the land, the season of joyful songs has come.

The cooing of the turtledove is heard in our land.

Come now, My love. My Yolanda, come.

Let Me see your face. And let Me hear your voice, for your voice is sweet and your face is beautiful.

Come now, My love, My lovely one, come." (Song of Solomon 2:10–13)

Six hours later her little leprous body was swept up into the furious love of her Abba. Later that same day, I learned from the staff that Yolanda was illiterate. She had never read the Bible, or any book for that matter, in her entire life. I surely had never repeated those words to her in any of my visits. I was, as they say, a man undone.[43]

Jesus is, in a word, *Astounding*.

He'll cross the sea and face the powers of death to save *one* man. He'll drop into a leper colony to share death with *one* woman. And he will go to hell and back to save *you*.

He is just that good.

And so when he asks you to take up a weapon and fight, you need to understand he may be calling you to save just *one* person. Perhaps it's a long-forgotten family member who you have a feeling may come back to God. Perhaps it's that lady you

---

43   Manning, *The Furious Longing of God*, 53–56.

see on the street every day on your way to work. Perhaps it's the guy who everyone jokes about at the office—the guy who just seems a little strange. Maybe there is a reason he's so strange and maybe your next mission is to find out why and introduce him to Christ. Perhaps your next mission is to go back to your husband, your wife, your son, or your daughter, and tell them that next time you're going to fight for *them*.

Whatever your mission may be, just know this one thing. Jesus the Magnificent rides into combat right next to you. And so what do you have to fear? He is the King after all.

Fight for the One, and the many will be saved.

Of course, no man fights alone—not even Christ—so let's take a look for a moment at how to choose your fellow warriors.

CHAPTER 11:
CHOOSING
MISSION MEN

DOUGLAS MACARTHUR WAS perhaps one of America's most revered military leaders. Much like our story, what made MacArthur such a grand character was not so much what he did in victory but what he did in defeat.

In late 1941, undermanned and understaffed, MacArthur was forced off the Philippines island chain by a superior Japanese Imperial force. During his escape, the general issued these famous words: "The president of the United States ordered me to break through the Japanese lines and proceed from Corregidor to Australia for the purpose, as I understand it, of organizing the American offensive against Japan, a primary objective of which is the relief of the Philippines. I came through and I shall return."[44]

Like a good military leader, MacArthur's next move was to rally a force behind him so he could return to the Philippines, release his men, and free the country he swore to protect. It took more than two years and involved several disputes with the leaders of the day, including a face-to-face meeting with the president.

MacArthur prevailed, and on December 20, 1944, his forces landed at Leyte Gulf in the Philippines. By the end of the day, his troops secured enough of the island to allow MacArthur and his staff to safely wade ashore. MacArthur's next words live in American history: "People of the Philippines: *I have returned.* By the grace of Almighty God our forces stand again on Philippine soil."[45]

When the World War II generals planned to fight a war, they first raised an army.

When Christ began planning for his war, he did the same: "And he went up on the mountain and called to him those whom he desired, and they came to him. And he appointed twelve (whom he also named apostles) so that they might be

44   Edward T. Imparato, *General MacArthur Speeches and Reports 1908–1964* (Nashville, TN: Turner, 2000), 124.

45   Douglas MacArthur, *Reminiscences of General of the Army Douglas MacArthur* (New York, NY: McGraw-Hill Book Co, 1964), 216.

with him and he might send them out to preach and have authority to cast out demons" (Mark 3:13–15).

God's plan for the restoration of the world essentially came down to a few things: a Man, some other men, a message, and a mission. Christ kicked off the campaign with three years of teaching and miracles. The purpose of these works was to train a band of strategically placed men (and women) for the work of the Kingdom. They were instructed daily and reminded constantly of his Word. They were commissioned to preach and to have authority not only of Israel but of the nations.

How well did Jesus accomplish his mission for raising an army?

Well, walk down the street of any major city and look in any direction. Chances are good you will see at least one church and probably more than one. The last statistic I saw said nearly 2 billion people currently call themselves Christians—and all that from one man gathering a few men to share a mission!

According to the previous text from Mark 3, the mission Christ gave his disciples was simple. They were to do three things very well: to be with Christ, to preach, and to cast out demons.

After the resurrection, you see one addition: "And Jesus came and said to them, 'All authority in heaven and on earth has been given to me. Go therefore and make disciples of all nations, baptizing them in the name of the Father and of the Son and of the Holy Spirit, teaching them to observe all that

I have commanded you. And behold, I am with you always, to the end of the age" (Matthew 28:18–20).

Jesus added the following criterion to the list: "make disciples."[46] It makes sense, too, because he was about to go to the Father; thus, the task of multiplication rested on his followers.

Sadly, we have long since surrendered the clarity of this mission.

How many times when you read a church's mission statement do you see these four things? Try just about never. Most mission statements, while they sound very exciting, fall quite short of this goal. Frankly, most sound more like *business* mission statements. My guess is well-meaning pastors would rather have it the other way; it's just that the real mission doesn't read very well.

Here are three church mission statements I have recently read:

> 1. Being desirous of promoting practical goodness in the world, and of aiding each other in our moral and religious improvement, we have associated ourselves together—not as agreeing in opinion, not as having attained universal truth in belief or

---

46   If you want to get picky, you could include baptizing and teaching to the list in Matthew 28. I am assuming this is included in the command to "make disciples" and is specific to the church. In this passage, making disciples seems to be the overall command.

perfection in character, but as seekers after truth and goodness.[47]

2. We gather together in love and fellowship to worship and foster spiritual growth, to serve humanity, and to understand ourselves and our universe.[48]

3. At _____ Church we're not about "having it all together" or even pretending we do. We're just a family trying to grow together toward a God who knows us and can help us put all the pieces of this sometimes bizarre world into perspective. We may not have all the answers but we know someone who does. In fact He not only knows the answers ... He made up the questions.[49]

Seriously, I'll bet you a hundred bucks your pastor would *love* to come to the next congregational meeting and instead of listing the things he has done in the last year (counseling, building programs, etc.), to simply say, "Well, basically my job is pretty straight forward. I spend a lot of time with God. That's always fun. I preach a lot. But then again you knew that. I cast out demons whenever I get the chance. And I make new disciples so I can work myself out of a job. That's pretty much it. Any questions?"

47   http://www.danielharper.org/blog/?p=1533

48   Ibid.

49   http://www.missionstatements.com/church_mission_statements.html

Needless to say, we have a long way to go until we accomplish Christ's mission. And to get there, our first step, much like MacArthur's and much like Christ's, is to find fellow warriors.

Your litmus test for choosing fellow warriors is fairly simple. You use Christ's criteria: find men (and women) who love to spend time with Jesus, who understand his Word, who cast out demons, and who make disciples.

Look for such men. Indeed, pray for such men. And once you find such men, train them and fight with them.

There is a great line in the movie *Band of Brothers* that comes when Easy Company was marching into Bastogne, the very center of the "battle of the bulge." While retreating U.S. forces were marching *out* of town, Easy Company was walking *into* town.

One of the retreating soldiers said, "Don't go in there, you'll be surrounded."

To that the Easy Company soldier replied, "We're paratroopers, we're used to being surrounded!"[50]

Six months later, Easy Company marched out of Bastogne victorious.

Being a man on a mission involves: discovering why God placed you on this earth, staying on that mission, taking risks, understanding that sometimes the mission is a man, and then finding fellow warriors to fight with you.

---

50   *Band of Brothers*, directed by Phil Alden Robinson, Richard Loncraine, Mikael Salomon, Tom Hanks, and David Leland (Glendale, CA: DreamWorks, 2001).

So, go right now and pray for that.

Ask God to begin to reveal what he has called you to do. Then execute your mission while simultaneously praying for fellow paratroopers, men and women who will gladly join you in the task of being surrounded by the enemy and *beating* them.

Then, and only then, start asking God for *authority* and *power*, which will be the subject of our next section.

SECTION 4:

CHRIST
THE
POWERFUL

Section 4:
Christ the Powerful

"Seated with the cosmic Christ, sharing his throne, is the cosmic Christian. As the cosmic Christ, He is Lord. He is God. As the cosmic Christian in Christ, I am a man of cosmic power. It is his power which operates within me."[51]

— Dr. Ed Murphy

"But from now on the Son of Man shall be seated at the right hand of the power of God."

— Luke 22:69

---

51   Dr. Ed Murphy, *The Handbook of Spiritual Warfare* (Nashville, TN: Thomas Nelson, 2003), 394.

A GREAT SCENE IN the middle of the movie *Braveheart* so cleverly mirrors our own leadership today that I would be remiss if I passed this up. In the thirteenth century, the Scottish nobles were basically a group of little pansies whose very existence was to bow before the English king in the hope of retaining their property and their comfort. Each time you see them in the movie, they are scheming and planning on how they might "negotiate" with the English. At times they dress like warriors, but don't be fooled; at heart, they are cowards.

When William Wallace comes to address the nobles, the big issue on the docket is which clan William will back as the true heir to the throne of Scotland. This is, of course, laughable because no one in Scotland actually had *rule* over anything in Scotland, or anywhere else on planet earth. Scotland's "king" was more or less a political lapdog to the king of England. What fun.

In this scene, William comes to speak to the nobles and to fight for the freedom of his people. He is dismayed at what he sees from the nobles and so he lets them have it: "You're so concerned with squabbling for the scraps from Longshanks's table that you've missed your God-given right to something better. There's a difference between us: You think the people of this country exist to provide you with position. I think your position exists to provide these people with freedom. And I go to make sure that they have it."[52]

It could not be a more appropriate analogy of the state of the Christian church today.

We have been called to rise up as warriors. We have been called to do what Adam did not do: take dominion and rule over the earth and subdue *all* of it to Christ. Instead we sit Indian style in little circles shielding our eyes from the sick, lame, deaf, and destitute. Instead of fighting for the Kingdom, we engage in petty land squabbles over things such as where to place the communion altar and how many ounces of wine should be in the communion cup, or whether the cup should actually be filled with grape juice instead.

I am not kidding. Go and read some of the most popular Christian blogs today, and your heart will simply drop. The theme is this: we have found the enemy, and the enemy is us! It's like a round robin of the most obscure doctrinal issues, one after the other. The voices are heated, and no one really changes their mind because no one really cares to. It's all just an escape from the real world, and it's a wonderful chance to say some nasty things under an anonymous screen name.

J. C. Ryle put it this way:

52   *Braveheart*, directed by Mel Gibson (London, UK: Icon Entertainment, 1995).

With whom is the Christian soldier meant to fight? *Not with other Christians.* Wretched indeed is that man's idea of religion who fancies that it consists in perpetual controversy. He who is never satisfied unless he is engaged in some strife between church and church, chapel and chapel, sect and sect, party and party, knows nothing as he ought to know. Never is the cause of sin so helped as when Christians waste their strength in quarrelling with one another, and spend their time in petty squabbles.[53]

I have been in churches where the biggest battles are about the music, which instruments are appropriate and which ones are not. I've seen an entire church newsletter devoted to the virtues of singing "a cappella" (without instruments). The author spent a page discussing how he would like to chop up every church piano into tiny pieces. I've listened to endless debates over the time of worship and the arrangement of chairs in the sanctuary. I've heard men rail one against the other over what age the children should be allowed to take communion. It's a meal, OK, and they are hungry.

Small men with *small* missions, fighting *small* battles.

Where is the William Wallace of today? Where is the *large* man with a *large* mission fighting *large* battles? Where, oh, where is the man who will fight for his family and the hearts of his children? Where is the man who will rise up to lead a company by biblical values of profit and community? Where is

---

53   J. C. Ryle, *Holiness* (Moscow, ID: Charles Nolan Publishing, 2011), 111.

the man who will run for political office *expressly* in the name of Christ and his coming kingdom?

Can't you just see the interview on CNN?

Biased-liberal-media-news-anchor: "What will you do in your first 100 days, Mr. Christian-Running-For-Election?"

Mr.Christian-Running-For-Election: "Well, that's simple. I am going to find out exactly how Christ rules his Kingdom; I am going to ask for his help; and then I am going to do exactly what he tells me."[54]

Biased-liberal-media-news-anchor [with a smirk]: "So... then you intend to let your Christian faith bias your decisions as president?"

Mr.Christian-Running-For-Election: "I would say so— very much so, yes. For example, I am planning on sleeping with my wife and no one else. I won't be taking any bribes. When I say I am going to do something, well, I am going to do it. I will fight for the orphan, the destitute, and the homeless. I will fight against the pimp, the pusher, and the human trafficker. I won't allow the government to steal anymore of your money (anything over 10% is asking for more than the church asks for and that's

---

54   I am not exaggerating this. Israel's King David was perhaps the finest ruler of all time. When he had a tough decision to make, the Bible says, "Then David inquired of the LORD...and the LORD said..." That idea of leaders calling on God is so lost on our society today that such a man would be branded a lunatic. And thus, we have the leaders we *deserve*.

just wrong). And so, yes, if that is what
you mean by 'biased,' I fully intend to let
my Christian faith bias my decisions as
president."

Oh, for such a man.

The desire to fight is so ingrained in the human heart
that we literally have no choice in the matter. God put it there,
so we *will* fight. We *all* fight. The choice we have is what to fight
for. Sadly, when the church does not fight its common cause, it
ends up fighting itself.

John Rushdoony puts it this way: "The urge to dominion
does not disappear simply because the church does not speak of
it. Instead, it reappears as an ugly and sinful struggle for power
in the church; rightful dominion being neglected or denied,
sinful dominion then begins to emerge. The life of the church
becomes then an ugly struggle over meaningless trifles in which
the sole purpose is sinful power and dominion."[55]

It is high time to drop our petty disputes and serve at
the King's court and at the King's bidding. It's time to release
anger, pride, and self-serving squabbles and join together to
engage our common enemy. It's time to get on line and call in
air support. The war has begun, and there is no more time for
inter-service rivalries.

---

55   Rushdoony, *Institutes of Biblical Law*, 450.

It is time for Christian men to heed the call and serve valiantly as husbands, fathers, business-owners, entrepreneurs, elders, and statesmen.

It is time to shelter the homeless, take in the orphan, feed the hungry, clothe the naked, heal the sick, cast out demons, and, yes, even raise the dead.

And finally, it is time to wield the Word of God, not as a weapon for internal struggle, but as a sword to bring light and life to a dark world under siege.

Who will heed such a call? Will you?

God has given his church both authority and power to accomplish its mission. When used improperly, it will kill a church. When used properly, it will change the world.

Conveniently, we move now into the book of Luke where the warrior theme is what occurs when a leader comes with both *authority* and *power*.

CHAPTER 12:
JESUS AND THE ONE-TWO PUNCH

TIMES WERE ACTUALLY quite similar back in first-century Palestine. Both political and religious leaders ruled the area we now know as Israel.

The political leaders were appointed by Caesar and were given a great deal of authority and power to subdue the land for Rome.

The religious leaders of Israel were also given authority by their position in the church, but to be fair, they were not all that comfortable with the authority part. Sure, they enjoyed the front-row seats at *Phantom of the Opera* and the complimentary desserts at Italian restaurants. They loved that people called them "holy men," even though they secretly knew they were not. And they definitely liked the cushy salary and benefits package that came with the job.

Just a bit, and maybe a bit more, but, of course, all in the name of the temple.

The classic doctrinal dispute in the first century was not about how to help the homeless. Instead, they argued about circumcision. In other words, men were more concerned about what was in their *pants* than who was in their pews.

But with all the power and prestige, these religious leaders did *not* appreciate that they had to take a stance on anything. And so they didn't. It was fairly common back then for a leader to stand up at the synagogue and simply quote the opinion of rabbi after rabbi after rabbi.

"Now...as for Moses and that Red Sea story. Rabbi Shems thought it happened this way, and of course Rabbi Moyle from the synagogue up in Bethlehem disagreed, but then again Rabbi Moyle disagreed with everything Rabbi Shems said." And on and on it went.

So when Christ came onto the scene in the first century, he entered a Jewish world with no real leaders, and certainly no men who *acted* like leaders. The problem was when you have authority, but you act like you don't, you are, in effect *giving* all your authority away—a point we will explore in more detail in a few minutes.

Christ showed up, and wham, the people were blown away because he spoke his own mind and his own words, and his bite was even harder than his bark.

As usual, we get the first hint of what's coming from John the Baptist. You will notice he zeroes in on Jesus' power: "John answered them all, saying, 'I baptize you with water, but he who is *mightier* than I is coming.'" (Luke 3:16).

You're impressed with the things I can do? John laughs. *Just wait until you meet my cousin Jesus!*

Then, on cue, Jesus hit the stage with a rare and disruptive combination of both power and authority. We find the first evidence of this right in the beginning of Luke. Jesus was in his hometown where he was asked to speak at the synagogue. The reading that day was about the coming Messiah.

Coincidence? I think not.

Instead of quoting nine different rabbis and the meat packer down the street, Jesus just looked up and, in effect, said, *So...you know that guy Isaiah's talking about right there—the one who's going to heal the blind and set people free? Well, I have some news for you. That's me! So, deal with it.*

"And he rolled up the scroll and gave it back to the attendant and sat down. And the eyes of all in the synagogue were fixed on him. And he began to say to them, 'Today this Scripture has been fulfilled in your hearing.' And all spoke well of him and marveled at the gracious words that were coming from his mouth" (Luke 4:20–22).

So far, so good. The sermon was going well, and the people were hanging on Jesus' every word. If he had only quit there, he would have been treated to a nice Jewish lunch and multiple downloads on SermonAudio.com. But, to be fair, Jesus really didn't care about their applause; he cared about their *hearts*. And for the life of him, he couldn't help but tell the truth. He knew his friends and neighbors would reject him sooner or later, so he might as well save a few right now.

> And he said, "Truly, I say to you, no prophet is acceptable in his hometown. But in truth, I tell you, there were many widows in Israel in the days of Elijah, when the heavens were shut up three years and six months, and a great famine came over all the land, and Elijah was sent to none of them but only to Zarephath, in the land of Sidon, to a woman who was a widow. And there were many lepers in Israel in the time of the prophet Elisha, and none of them was cleansed, but only Naaman the Syrian." When they heard these things, all in the synagogue were filled with wrath. And they rose up and drove him out of the town and brought him to the brow of the hill on which their town was built, so that they could throw him down the cliff. But passing through their midst, he went away. (Luke 4:24–30)

Jesus basically told his entire hometown that because they wouldn't believe in him, they were toast. He wasn't going to put on a show, and he wasn't doing any tricks. Their unbelief would be their downfall.

Honestly, this whole "Jesus as Messiah" thing had to be difficult for the hometown folks. They knew Jesus since he was three. They saw him fall off his bike, they saw him scuff his knee, and they saw him learning how to throw a spiral. And now, not only did Jesus, Mary's own son, just call himself the Messiah, but he didn't quote anyone...except himself!

As you can imagine, the people went crazy. The whole gang promptly left the synagogue and attempted to throw Jesus off a cliff. Jesus was unimpressed. He simply passed right through the crowd.

That is what happens when you have both authority and power. You get things done. And you enrage the establishment. Jesus' first sermon did both. The people were blown away by his teaching, which came with authority. But they were also infuriated by his honesty—a trait so rarely seen in their leaders that the people just couldn't deal with it in Jesus.

Jesus left Nazareth in the dust, literally. He took his power and authority north to the town of Capernaum, where even against the best advice of his "ministry consultants," he walked into another synagogue: "He went down to Capernaum, a city of Galilee. And he was teaching them on the Sabbath, and they were astonished at his teaching, for his word possessed *authority*" (Luke 4:31–32).

The folks in Capernaum obviously took a lot closer look at Jesus than did the folks from his hometown. And what impressed them the most was the same thing that initially impressed the people of Nazareth: Jesus spoke with authority.

It's as though the words came right from his own mind, his own heart (because, of course, they did). But Jesus knew authority alone was insufficient. He could speak as if he was in charge, but he actually needed to *be* in charge, and that took *power*. It was right there, almost as if on cue, a demon-possessed man strutted into the synagogue.

> And in the synagogue there was a man who had the spirit of an unclean demon, and he cried out with a loud voice, "Ha! What have you to do with us, Jesus of Nazareth? Have you come to destroy us? I know who you are—the Holy One of God." But Jesus rebuked him, saying, "Be silent and come out of him!" And when the demon had thrown him down in their midst, he came out of him, having done him no harm. And they were all amazed and said to one another, "What is this word? For with *authority and power* he commands the unclean spirits, and they come out!" And reports about him went out into every place in the surrounding region. (Luke 4:33–37, emphasis mine)

This was the perfect one-two power punch. Christ's authority opened their hearts, and his power dropped them to their knees. And, believe it or not, the same can be true for you and me.

Let's start with authority.

CHAPTER 13:
THE AUTHORITY
PATTERN

AUTHORITY IS THE God-appointed position of dominion over, above, or in charge of something or someone. For a father or mother, your authority is over your family, land, home, vehicles, and finances. For a business leader, your authority is over the people, property, and profits assigned to you. For a governmental leader, your authority is over the region you have been elected to preside over. For a pastor or elder, your authority is over the people in your church.

In all cases, your mission is to rule them well, as Christ did.

Dallas Willard writes, "Our 'kingdom' is simply the range of our effective will. Whatever we genuinely have say over is in our kingdom. And our having the say over something is precisely what places it within our kingdom. In creating human beings God made them to rule, to reign, to have dominion in a limited sphere. Only so they can be persons. Any being that has say over nothing at all is no person."[56]

Now I will admit, this type of rulership is rarely taught and seldom embraced in the average church today. Far too often, you find believers cowering in the corner and waiting, yes hoping even, for the rapture so they can get the heck out of here and onto something better. Oh, and as for work, property, and ownership, those are necessary, indeed, but only a necessary *evil*—something we must endure while we wait for our future home in the clouds or wherever.

We shy away from authority, and we certainly shy away from using the word "authority." Honestly, when is the last time you heard a church leader say he had "authority over the church"? We don't like that word because we have all lived with people who used their authority for evil purposes. But, rightly understood, authority is like sex, beer, and chocolate. There can be a right use for authority and a wrong use for authority. It's what you do with your authority that counts.

The point is simple: you have been given authority. No matter what you choose to believe, that fact is as true as the

---

56   Willard, *The Divine Conspiracy*, 21-22.

day is long. The key then is to understand that one of only two things will happen with your authority:

Authority either *grows* or it is *given away*.

If you rule like Christ ruled and use your authority for good, you will get more authority and do more good.

And if you rule like Adam ruled, your God-given authority will slip right out of your hands and right into the hands of another ruler of this world, the evil one. Once that happens, life truly gets difficult.

In Luke, Jesus told a story that accurately reflects what happens when you are given authority. Here is how the story starts: "He said therefore, 'A nobleman went into a far country to receive for himself a kingdom and then return. Calling ten of his servants, he gave them ten minas, and said to them, "Engage in business until I come"'" (Luke 19:12–13).

Just to understand the context, Jesus told this story on the way to Jerusalem where he would soon be murdered. Thus, the nobleman in the story, the one who was going away, was Jesus. What he was saying, in effect, was he was going away, and he was going to give his disciples something he expected them to multiply.

> "When he returned, having received the kingdom, he ordered these servants to whom he had given the money to be called to him, that he might know what they had gained by doing business. The first came before him, saying, 'Lord, your mina has made ten minas more.' And he said to him, 'Well done, good servant! Because you have been faithful in a

very little, you shall have authority over ten cities.' And the second came, saying, 'Lord, your mina has made five minas.' And he said to him, 'And you are to be over five cities.' Then another came, saying, 'Lord, here is your mina, which I kept laid away in a handkerchief; for I was afraid of you, because you are a severe man. You take what you did not deposit, and reap what you did not sow.' He said to him, 'I will condemn you with your own words, you wicked servant! You knew that I was a severe man, taking what I did not deposit and reaping what I did not sow? Why then did you not put my money in the bank, and at my coming I might have collected it with interest?' And he said to those who stood by, 'Take the mina from him, and give it to the one who has the ten minas.' And they said to him, 'Lord, he has ten minas!' I tell you that to everyone who has, more will be given, but from the one who has not, even what he has will be taken away." (Luke 19:15–26)

I know, I know, it's not fair, right? I mean that one guy already had ten minas and Jesus gave him even more. That doesn't sound right, does it? It doesn't sound fair at all.

That is until you view this as an investing illustration, which of course it is. Imagine you have three different stockbrokers and you give each one $10,000. After a year, the first broker gives you $100,000 back (a ten-times return on your investment). The second gives you $50,000 back (a five-times return). And the third dodges your phone calls for a full year and then finally admits, "Yeah, I really didn't do anything with your money. I was too busy playing golf."

So let me ask you: which broker will get your entire portfolio next year?

Answer: the one who gave you back a hundred grand.

And the same is true for the kingdom of God. That is precisely the point of the parable in Luke. Jesus has given you authority. It's what you do with that authority that counts. You can either use it wisely, creating a massive return on his investment, or you can squander it. In other words, you can grow it or you can give it away.

Remember, when I say authority, I mean about homes, cars, finances, kids, employees, stock accounts, churches, businesses, sports teams. Basically, I am talking about *everything*. That's because everything on planet earth belongs to someone here on planet earth.

There have always been two options, and the choice is yours. What will you do with your authority? Will you choose to rule well and see your authority grow? Or will you release your authority and see it stolen from you?

The choice is yours and you have two examples to follow: Adam or Christ.

Let's take a look at the decisions they each made with authority.

CHAPTER 14:
THE MAN WHO
LOST IT ALL

THERE IS A movement in Christianity that makes little sense in its context. You hear this just about everywhere you go. It's the belief that if we could only get back to Eden, all would be well. If only we could get back to the purity and the sinlessness of the garden before the fall, then, and only then will we be truly free.

But seen as a part of the big biblical picture, this desire for a return to Eden is a ridiculous attempt to go backward to a time that was transitory in nature.

And here's why.

Even though Eden is far preferable to what we experience today, the entire movement of biblical (and human) history has always been a movement *forward*. The Bible story starts with a garden. It ends with a garden city. It begins with pure and undefiled man set in the midst of a cosmic battle. It ends with pure and undefiled man victorious over an enemy put to death.

Our problem is we view Eden as the destination. But even for Adam, Eden was never the destination; it was only a stop on the way to the new heavens and the new earth.

The words in Genesis 1, "In the beginning," refer to the beginning of the universe as we know it. But the biblical story tells of another beginning, one that existed in eternity past. We find that "beginning" in John: "In the beginning was the Word, and the Word was with God, and the Word was God. He was in the beginning with God" (John 1:1–2).

[Insert a very long pause here.]

"All things were made through him, and without him was not anything made that was made" (John 1:3).

In the beginning, the real beginning, there were three—the Father, the Son, and the Holy Spirit—perfect in unity and being. Here we witness purity, holiness, and purpose. Sin had not yet entered the picture, nor had rebellion. The Trinity existed before the creation of the angels, the world, or man.

Sin and rebellion first came into the picture not at Genesis 3 but long before Adam ever entered the picture. Rebellion actually existed first in heaven. That happened when Satan, the most splendid of all angels—the guardian of the glory of God—decided his station as chief angel was insufficient.

We find this passage in Isaiah 14. The prophet is speaking poetically about the king of Babylon, but many scholars agree that the imagery is drawn primarily from an account of Satan's fall,[57]

"How you are fallen from heaven,

O Day Star, son of Dawn!

How you are cut down to the ground,

you who laid the nations low!

You said in your heart,

'I will ascend to heaven;

above the stars of God

I will set my throne on high;

I will sit on the mount of assembly

in the far reaches of the north;

I will ascend above the heights of the clouds;

I will make myself like the Most High.'"

(Isaiah 14:12–14, emphasis mine)

Long before the creation of Eden, Satan chose rebellion. His goal (as ridiculous as this may sound) was to dethrone

---

[57]   Again, the analogy is drawn from the prophesy against the king of Babylon and most likely refers back to Satan's fall. Incidentally, the idea of "becoming like God" or of even overtaking his throne to rule was not a new concept to Isaiah's audience. It started with Satan's heavenly rebellion, made its way to earth in the fall of Adam (Genesis 3:5), continued in the story of Genesis (Genesis 11:4), and even continues to this very day. All sin is, in essence, an attempt to overthrow God's rule and claim his throne for our own.

God and become the ruler of everything. The result was both predictable and tragic. Satan enlisted an army, taking one-third of the angels, and brought war to the very courts of heaven. The Almighty prevailed (of course), and Satan was cast down along with his fellow warriors.

Dismayed, but not totally defeated, Satan then shifted his strategy.

Forget for a moment, the imagery in the following passage, and just notice what Satan chose to do upon his defeat: "And I saw a beast rising out of the sea, with ten horns and seven heads, with ten diadems on its horns and blasphemous names on its heads.... [I]t was allowed to make war on the saints and to conquer them. And authority was given it over every tribe and people and language and nation" (Revelation 13:1, 7).

Satan knew he could not prevail over God. He tried that once and it failed miserably. So he changed his tactics and chose to wage war against the closest thing to God he could find—the very image of God on earth, namely humankind.

No wonder Adam fell.

He was given authority over a perfect and spotless world, undefiled and unspoiled. Yet that same world was set in the midst of the greatest battle in the history of the cosmos. God, in his infinite wisdom, chose to create Adam as his warrior for earth.

Adam's mission was simple: he must fight...and he must win.

History tells of the tragic result.

Instead of choosing to obey his Captain, Adam listened to the voice of the enemy. Instead of trusting God, Adam chose to trust the voice of the accuser. Adam fell and all of creation fell with him. His fall gave Satan dominion over the earth. That's because Adam *gave his authority away* through sin.

Thankfully, by his grace, God had a backup plan. With Adam's fall arose the need for one greater than Adam to rise and fight for what was lost. God volunteered for the suicide mission. He became a man, lived a perfect life, suffered, died, and rose again.

Christ's victory took the world back. On the day Christ rose from the dead, he re-established his ownership, authority, and dominion over the Earth.

Once again, Christ owned it *all.*

Now, here is something utterly remarkable: upon re-gaining, re-winning, and re-establishing his authority on earth, Christ did the un-believable:

He gave it all back to us.[58]

To make sure no question was in anyone's mind, Christ chose his last sentences on earth very carefully. You've heard it called the Great Commission. I call it the *Great Dominion.*

> Now the eleven disciples went to Galilee, to the mountain to which Jesus had directed them. And when they saw him they worshiped him, but some doubted. And Jesus came and said to them, "All *authority* in heaven and on earth has been

---

[58] Credit to John Eldredge and Gary North for introducing me to this concept.

given to me. Go therefore and make disciples of all nations, baptizing them in the name of the Father and of the Son and of the Holy Spirit, teaching them to observe all that I have commanded you. And behold, I am with you always, to the end of the age." (Matthew 28:16–20, emphasis mine)

Gary North says this: "Satan in principle lost his Adam-given authority the day Christ died. Christians re-inherited it in principle the day Christ rose from the dead."[59]

I know for a fact I would not do what Christ did. I have a pretty long memory and a fairly short fuse. If you betray me once, chances are you're not getting a second chance. But instead of holding a grudge, Jesus gave us a second shot.

This is the kind of backward logic that makes God, well, God. He turned the best advice of his heavenly cabinet around and laughingly exclaims, "Now watch this!" If he had advisors (which he didn't), they would have told him to never, ever give authority back to the people. "You already tried that before, God. And so for the sake of all that is right, you must now and forever maintain the centrality of a strong central government. Tax the rich and feed the poor and many such things."

"Forget feeding the poor," God smiles. "Let's just make them rich again!"

He is enough to fall in love with ten times over.

Frankly, there was no way anyone could justify giving us authority back. It's hard enough finding our underwear drawer in the morning, much less ruling the earth. But then again, Jesus

---

59   Gary North, *Liberating Planet Earth*, 27.

the Conqueror did not worry too much about our weakness. That's because he knew we would forever have a trump card to use against our enemy, even in the midst of the hardest days. We have the presence and the power of Christ himself!

So what is our new mission on earth? Here you go: exercise our authority and crush Satan.

See how Paul states it in the book of Romans: "The God of peace will soon crush Satan under your feet" (Romans 16:20).

Notice Paul didn't say God would crush Satan under *Christ's* feet; he said he will crush Satan under *your* feet. It's basically the same thing. That's because you are his body... and you are his feet, hands, and strength. God was, in effect, commanding you to fight so you may secure *his* victory.

The crazy part is that apparently he did it all for love. Not because of his love for us, which is great enough indeed, but so that, once again, we would have the opportunity to use our dominion well, and use it to love *him*.

Doesn't this one fact alone make you want to love him all the more? Doesn't it motivate you to use your God-given authority well?

Now, here is the tricky part. Authority is only one-half of the equation. Jesus knew that to accomplish our new mission of authority we would need power. It is impossible to rule without it.

So let's see how we can get that kind of power.

CHAPTER 15:

THE POWER PATTERN

M Y WIFE WAS sick the other night, and I needed to get to the drugstore for medicine. The speed limit in my town is 35 miles per hour. I was going 46. The second I saw the police car I knew I was busted. In fact, even before he turned on his lights, I started pulling into a parking lot.

Then I proceeded to talk myself out of a $200 ticket. In fact, I have a formula for talking my way out of tickets that works pretty much every time. Want to know what it is? (OK, send $19.95 and a self-addressed, stamped envelope to P.O. Box... never mind, I'll just tell you.)

Here you go: *I agree profusely*. That's it.

Here is how the conversation went the other night:

Cop: "Do you know why I pulled you over?"

Me: "Yes, sir, I do, I was going 46 miles per hour, and the speed limit here is 35. I was definitely going well past the speed limit."

Cop: "Do you live near here?"

Me: "Yes, sir, I live right up the hill. Honestly, I know better. I've driven this road a thousand times."

(My favorite line is coming up next and I know it.)

Cop: "OK, I am going to go ahead and let you off with a warning. Just take it a bit slower next time."

Me: "You're a good man, officer; be safe tonight, OK?"[60]

Like Billy Dee Williams used to say, "It works every time."

So here is the point. We are talking about authority and power. The police officer who pulled me over had both. The authority was pinned to his shirt. We call it a badge. It doesn't matter how fast the officer drives in his spare time, when he is wearing his badge, he is allowed to pull cars over. He is granted that authority from a higher source. But authority alone doesn't do the trick. The city backs it up by giving the officer some

---

60   Don't send me cranky letters about the importance of obeying the law. I know I am supposed to drive the speed limit. It's just that once you've flown 950 miles per hour in a jet, 35 is very, very s-l-o-o-o-o-w.

power too. That night, he had a gun, a nightstick, and some mace.

Even if I wanted to, I wasn't going to mess with him.

Now, imagine how ridiculous a police officer would look if instead of carrying those three lethal weapons, he carried a plastic water gun, a twig, and a can of Silly String.

Expected survival on the street = five minutes.

It is, once again, a perfect analogy of the church today. Without power, our expected survival time in spiritual combat is microscopic.

The crazy thing is, much like the city, God has given the church immense amounts of power. We should be able to move mountains (literally) if they get in the way of the Kingdom. But instead of grabbing a gun and making believers, we go to war with Silly String. Instead of throwing mountains, we throw sticks.

It's a wonder we get anything done.

The church has authority. So do the people in the church. That far we have already covered. However to properly wield that authority and to fight well, we need power and we need to use it. While there is no hard-and-fast formula, there does seem to be a pattern for how to get, keep, and wield that kind of power.[61] The model is demonstrated, once again, by the life

---

61   I purposely use the word "pattern" instead of "formula" or "recipe." That's precisely because rarely do you ever find a hard-and-fast spiritual formula for almost anything in the Bible. For example, military strategy is sound—and it works most of the time—but every once in a while, God tells us to do the very opposite of the "pattern." Like walking around a city for seven days. Sure, God uses means,

of Christ. Here is the first part: "And Jesus, full of the Holy Spirit, returned from the Jordan and was led by the Spirit in the wilderness for forty days, being tempted by the devil. And he ate nothing during those days. And when they were ended, he was hungry" (Luke 4:1–2).

You are familiar with this scene. Jesus swung by to see Cousin John and, while there, got baptized. As soon as he came out of the water, he was filled with the Holy Spirit, who summarily led him into the wilderness. During that time, Jesus was surrounded by wild animals, he found water where he could, but he ate nothing—not even a small handful of berries (however tempting that may have been).

During these forty days of fasting, Jesus essentially spent the majority of his time in communion with his Father—we call it prayer. When the forty days was over, Satan appeared and tempted Christ at least three times. Jesus resisted the temptations valiantly, and Satan was sent away to come back another day.

Score one for the good guys.

Now, it is commonly understood that Jesus' not eating food for forty days served to weaken him—to make him more susceptible to temptation number one: turning stones into

---

and there seems to be some fairly straightforward principles that work most of the time. But then again, God also breaks with the principles from time to time to serve his own purposes. Normally, power comes from prayer, fasting, and obedience, but then again, Christ gave power to his followers at times even without all that. All that to say, follow the biblical patterns, but expect a curveball every once in a while too.

bread. Quite to the contrary, when we take a biblical view of fasting, we see that, in effect, these forty days of self-denial served to *strengthen* Jesus spiritually, even as it weakened him physically. Additionally, the extended time spent in prayer served to clothe him with even more power. By the time Satan showed up, Christ, having fasted and prayed for forty days, was so full of spiritual power, drawing strength from his one-on-one communion with God, the devil literally did not stand a chance.

Now, here is the interesting part. At the beginning of the forty days, the Bible says Jesus was "full of the Holy Spirit." At the end of forty days and after the temptation, Luke records the following (notice the subtle shift in words): "And Jesus returned in the power of the Spirit to Galilee, and a report about him went out through all the surrounding country. And he taught in their synagogues, being glorified by all" (Luke 4:14–15).

The difference is slight but, oh, so important. Jesus went into the wilderness *with the Spirit*; he returned *in the power of the Spirit*. From what we read in the text, that kind of power came liberally as a result of three simultaneous actions: fasting, prayer, and obedience.

Something supernatural occurs when you fast (i.e., don't eat or drink anything but water). I can't explain it, but it is a spiritual fact nonetheless. The effect is multiplied when you dedicate an additional amount of time to prayer during your fast. The effect is multiplied even further if you focus an additional amount of energy on obedience.[62]

That's the power pattern: prayer, fasting, and obedience. It's pretty simple, but then again, who wants to miss a meal, right? And that's why it's pretty rare too. But then again, it's also rare to find people in our churches who have real power. Maybe that's a clue; it's time for us to get back to the nature of true prayer and real fasting.

I don't have the time or the inclination to discuss all of the how and why on fasting and prayer; suffice it to say, I have included several resources in the back of the book.

I will, however, mention this. While it is not a commandment, Jesus assumed fasting was a normal part of the Christian life. That's probably why it is not mentioned all that much in the New Testament. Fasting was a given. Here is how Jesus discussed fasting: "And when you fast, do not look gloomy like the hypocrites, for they disfigure their faces that their fasting may be seen by others. Truly, I say to you, they have received their reward" (Matthew 6:16).

Notice Jesus did not say, "if you fast." He said, "when you fast." The difference is important. He assumed we were going to do it.

---

62   I'm not a huge fan of laying down hard-and-fast, you-must-do-this-or-else principles. That's because everyone is different and everyone is in a different stage of life. For example, if you are single, you may be able to fast once a week (maybe more). If you are the mom of a four-month-old, you may go six years before you get a quiet moment to pray, much less fast. So, go easy on yourself because Jesus does. Simply apply the principles to the best of your ability. Start small and work for more.

So...do it.

Before we move past fasting and prayer, I want to give you one very important warning: when you start to fast and pray, expect it to be opposed. You have an enemy who hates the fact you just read the previous two pages of this book. He is afraid of what might occur if you step into your God-given power. He would like for nothing else than to make you forget, disregard, or dismiss what I just told you to do. So, I'm going to put it straight: the first few times you take a swing at fasting and prayer *will* be difficult. Expect temptation. Expect distraction. Expect to get hit by stuff you don't normally get hit by. Expect it. It will happen.

Let me give you an example. One of my personal disciplines is to get at least one full day every month out of the office to connect with the Father and pray. I have found hiking to be the best way for me to get this done right. That way I can get away from e-mail, turn my phone off, and just *be* with the Father. I usually take my Bible, my journal, and some water.

My experience with spiritual attack during prayer hikes is so common it's almost laughable. Here is how it usually goes. Inevitably, for the first twenty minutes of the hike, I battle distraction.

Don't forget, you need to call Drew tomorrow.

Faith's ballet class is at six. Make sure you're home in time for that.

Hmmm. I wonder what we're having for dinner tomorrow night.

Some distraction is the natural effect of the fast pace of everyday life. You really do need to let your mind "wind down" so you can be still. However, much of the distraction is from the enemy.

I find it particularly helpful during distraction attacks to pray out loud. It helps you know when your mind is on the Father and when it is off. It also helps to pray against the distraction. Try this: "Father, I bring the full work of Christ against distraction. I choose to be still and know that you are God. Please clear my mind and allow me to focus on you."

Say that (or something close to it) out loud, and if you need to, say it over and over. Eventually, after some fighting, you will win and the fog will clear.

The next twenty minutes to an hour of my hikes are predictable as well. That's when the temptation really comes in strong. I usually start to get hit with some vile stuff—things I would never have thought of all by myself. One time, I was hiking along a trail to a 2,700-foot ridge here in San Diego. Just then I heard some female voices over the next ridge. I kid you not; my next thought was, "Hey, maybe there is a nudist colony over there. Maybe I should go over and check it out." It's ridiculous. And no, there was no nudist colony, and no I did not go check it out.

What I did was stop for a minute and ask this question, "Who has a vested interest in getting me off my spiritual game plan for today?"

Answer: the enemy, the spiritual forces at work against my freedom.

So, for about the next thirty minutes, I prayed against lust, adultery, and temptation. It did not disappear right away (these are rebellious spirits, after all). But after some battle, I won and, like a fog, it lifted.

Your temptation may be different. Most of what comes your way is perfectly tailored to you and your weakness. A pastor friend of mine gets hit with pain. He is a self-admitted hypochondriac and his idol is health. So, the temptation that comes when he gets alone with God often starts with a pain— in his side, in his neck, or in his head. It is all just a clever way to get him sidetracked from the main battle. If he gives in, the day with God is over and the enemy has won. If he fights, he'll win.

For me, once I battled distraction and temptation, the rest of the afternoon was spectacular. I walked one-on-one and conversationally with the living God. We talked about my current job, my calling, my family, and my future. We talked about others too. All in all, it was like breathing a giant breath of fresh air.

The icing on the cake came just as I cleared the trail near my car. Out of the blue I heard God say,

I had a good time with you today.[63]

---

[63] Note: this was not an audible voice. It wasn't like Obi-Wan Kenobi telling Luke to switch off his targeting computer before bombing the Death Star. But it *was* God speaking nonetheless, with his still, small voice. See the final pages of the book for resources on how to better communicate with God.

I was moved beyond words. It's unspeakable in its beauty that the God who flung the stars and hung the planets would want to go on a hike with me.

To summarize this brief excursion from the power discussion, just remember the warning. When you choose to pray, fast, and spend time with the Father, you will get opposition. Fight this. The result is worth it. And the breakthrough on the other side is spectacular.

We see how the disciples got slammed by this kind of spiritual distraction at the end of the Gospel of Luke. It was the night after the Last Supper and the night before the crucifixion. Jesus needed that extra five-hour energy shot of power from the Father, so he brought three friends along to the garden to pray with him. Just before Jesus headed up into the olive grove, he told his disciples, "Pray that you may not enter into temptation" (Luke 22:40).

Jesus then walked about as far as you could chuck a rock, about thirty yards maybe, and began to pour his heart out to God. We are talking about earnest, passionate prayer. He would need it. The temptations Jesus faced over the subsequent twenty-four hours were more than any man could stand alone, even the Son of God.

The camera now shifted to the boys down the hill, and all we see are big mounds of snoring men. It seems a few glasses of wine and a loaf of bread have taken their effect. The disciples were all passed out asleep on the hill—faces in the dirt, drool on their chins, left legs twitching ever so slightly. Jesus woke them up and told them once again, "Rise and pray that you may not enter into temptation" (Luke 22:46).

Well, we know the rest of the story. The soldiers came and all the disciples ran like scared children, despite their multiple promises to the contrary. Peter's actions were commendable at the start. He really did give it his best shot, but only a few hours later, he folded like a cocktail umbrella.

Presumably, had they listened to Jesus and prayed, they would not have betrayed Jesus that night. At the very least, they would have served as understanding and helpful friends to the suffering Christ-Man.

This from Dallas Willard:

> Peter and the other disciples would not in their moment of need have the ability to stand fast in the confrontation with Christ's enemies. But *had* they watched and prayed, as they were advised, the requisite ability would have been there when it was needed. They would have been in a condition of body and mind to secure the Father's assistance to stand as firmly as Jesus himself did. Here as always—whether in our natural life or in our spiritual life—the mark of a disciplined person is that they are able to do what needs to be done when it needs to be done.[64]

Finally, there is the question of why, exactly, God uses the disciplines of fasting, prayer, and obedience to give us power.

64   Dallas Willard, *Spirit of the Disciplines* (New York, NY: Harper Collins, 1990), 151.

Why couldn't he just use fasting and prayer, or for that matter, why doesn't he just give us power without all that?

The answer seems fairly straightforward: obedient character is a prerequisite for wielding power. A chainsaw is a cruel gift for a three-year-old boy. Sure, he may want it, and he may rejoice at receiving it. But he will likely kill himself or the family pet in the endeavor. God-given power assumes character. God is too wise to place power in the hands of immature men. And so he waits patiently until we have the character to wield his strength as a mature warrior.

We have all seen far too many examples of what happens when power ends up in the wrong hands. Hitler, Stalin, and for that matter, a long list of American presidents come to mind. Great power is a curse for a small man, as well as for the people he leads. As the saying goes, "Power corrupts. And absolute power corrupts absolutely." The only exception to that rule is God and those to whom he entrusts his power.

Let me put this as clearly as I can. Don't ask for power without simultaneously asking for the character to wield that power. Asking for character usually means suffering, the normal God-appointed means for developing Christian maturity. And because of that, we are often afraid to even ask for it. But don't be. God is good and he will give you what you need to endure.

Dallas Willard puts it this way,

> Finally, there is power to work the works of the kingdom. One of the most shocking statements Jesus ever made, and once again was in his "commencement address," was that "those who

rely on me shall do the works that I do, and even greater ones" (John 14:12). Perhaps we feel baffled and incompetent before this statement. But let us keep in mind that the world we live in desperately needs such works to be done. They would not just be for show or to impress ourselves or others. But, frankly, even a moderate-size "work" is more than most people's lives could sustain. One good public answer to our prayer might be enough to lock some of us into weeks of spiritual superiority. Great power requires great character if it is be a blessing and not a curse, and that character is something we only grow toward.[65]

Between us, this one point is my biggest personal issue when it comes to this book. You see, I really do want to see this message change the world. If the church at large embraces this message, it will change the world. The problem is, being perfectly honest, I am quite sure I don't yet have the character to sustain this power myself. To be sure, I am praying for it. It's just that I find myself often taking two steps backward after every step forward. Can you relate? The good news is Jesus is not done with me yet, inasmuch as he is not done with you yet. I agree with Paul: "Wretched man that I am! Who will deliver me from this body of death? Thanks be to God through Jesus Christ our Lord!" (Romans 7:24–25).

So I am praying both for more power and for more character.

---

65   Ibid., 368.

The principles are again so simple. The key to spiritual power is threefold: fasting, prayer, and obedience. If you want the kind of power Jesus had, the casting-out-demons-and-healing-the-sick kind of power, that's the normal biblical pattern.

The key, of course, is to actually *do* it.

The great news is when prayer, fasting, and obedience have sharpened your character, God is going to give you a lot of power. That's because you really can do the kind of things Jesus did, a concept we will now cover.

CHAPTER 16:

YOU CAN HAVE HIS POWER TOO

W E ARE ALL in agreement. Jesus was powerful. The point we often fail to grasp is how much power he has actually given to us. Frankly, the church at large has been so devoid of power for so long, it is natural for us to believe we never had it in the first place. And then there are the ridiculous displays of fake power we see on late-night televangelist networks. All this serves to encourage the church to shy away from the possibility of true power.

The enemy has been masterful in this regard, and his strategy has been executed almost without a flaw. Satan stands to lose a lot of ground when the church finally steps into its power. So he's convinced us works like healing, miracles, discernment, and the like are just weird things done by weird people. He's told us this power is not acceptable for "enlightened Christians." No, that would be improper. And, of course, being proper is quite biblical indeed, or so we have been led to believe.

I actually once attended a church whose members believed the gifts of the Spirit ceased to exist once the Bible was complete, around AD 70. These folks call themselves "cessationists." To be fair, they are well-meaning Christians. They rightly react against the silly late-night false power displays. The problem is they have swung the pendulum so far in the other direction they officially dispute any miraculous power. Worse, they attempt to back up their stance with Scripture. Their biblical evidence is sketchy at best and usually involves one of two arguments.

The first argument is a big stretch on 1 Corinthians 13. They believe Paul said prophecy (and spiritual gifts) would cease but that love would be around forever. The key here is to view the larger picture. In fact, we only have to go back one chapter to see what Paul thinks about spiritual gifts of power: "And God has appointed in the church first apostles, second prophets, third teachers, then miracles, then gifts of healing, helping, administrating, and various kinds of tongues. Are all apostles? Are all prophets? Are all teachers? Do all work miracles? Do all possess gifts of healing? Do all speak with tongues? Do all interpret? But earnestly desire the higher gifts" (1 Corinthians 12:28–31).

The record of Scripture and the 2,000-year history of the Christian church demonstrate quite the opposite of the "cessationist" viewpoint: when the people of God walk in obedience, God gives them power.

Their second justification for the absence of "gifts" is it makes the church look unorganized. That argument usually sounds something like this: "That could get a little hokie" (a pastor actually said that to me).

Oh really? Can you imagine this same reaction in the first century?

Listen, Jesus, I know you are going to heal that blind man over there. I can see that by the fact you are making mud puddles. Well, we need to talk. A bunch of the Pharisees got upset last time you healed someone. They said you were being "hokie."

Here's something to consider for the crowd who thinks God stopped speaking and doing miracles back in the first century. In the Bible, the *one* group that always got upset at healing was the *Pharisees.*

Bill Johnson is the pastor of Bethel Church in Redding, California, a congregation known well for its power. Here is what he says about his reaction to leaders who deny power:

> Many years ago a notable leader in the Body of Christ told me he had consciously gotten rid of the prophetic ministry in his church. He felt there was too much danger and too many potential problems. I respected him too much to voice my

disagreement, but I quietly got excited in my heart because in the natural, counterfeiters don't make pennies; it's not worth the effort. I knew that if the enemy worked that hard to create a counterfeit, the original must have great value. Only things of eternal consequence are worth the devil's attention.[66]

Jesus apparently wasn't worried about either he or his followers looking "hokie." Multiple examples are throughout the New (and Old) Testament of his followers using power. And it's clear these were not exceptions. Power followed those who followed Christ. One such example, can be found in Luke 9, when Jesus sent out the twelve apostles: "And he called the twelve together and gave them power and authority over all demons and to cure diseases, and he sent them out to proclaim the kingdom of God and to heal" (Luke 9:1–2).

But Jesus did not stop with the twelve. Just to make sure we don't get sidetracked into thinking power belonged only to those men, and those men now dead, Jesus sent his disciples again. Only this time, he sent seventy-two of them. Here is the result: "The seventy-two returned with joy, saying, 'Lord, even the demons are subject to us in your name!' And he said to them, 'I saw Satan fall like lightning from heaven. Behold, I have given you authority to tread on serpents and scorpions, and over all the power of the enemy, and nothing shall hurt you'" (Luke 10:17–19).

66   Johnson, *Dreaming with God*, 150.

Presumably, these were regular folks, just like you, me, Peter, John, and Martha. They were builders, bakers, and beauticians—the kid with multiple sclerosis, the guy who just found out his wife cheated on him, and probably the former town whore. These weren't super heroes. Heck, we don't even know their names. And yet these young believers were clothed with so much power Jesus witnessed the very defeat of Satan.

Now that's what I call power—and apparently in the hands of some very untrained people. We know that because they started to get carried away: "And he sent messengers ahead of him, who went and entered a village of the Samaritans, to make preparations for him. But the people did not receive him, because his face was set toward Jerusalem. And when his disciples James and John saw it, they said, 'Lord, do you want us to tell fire to come down from heaven and consume them?'" (Luke 9:52–54).

This cracks me up. Jesus wanted to find a place to sleep, and the town blew him off. James and John wouldn't stand for it. They asked if it was OK if they went "Sodom and Gomorrah" on the town. The strategic strike would presumably include hell, fire, brimstone, and close-air-support from a division of F-18s. *That will teach them not to mess with our Christ. That's right—take that!*

Now here is the interesting part: they thought they could do it. Honestly, can you imagine being so powerful that, if you wanted to, you could call down fire from heaven and smite an entire town? (I love that word—*smite*).

Well, it's possible. This kind of power is supposed to be the norm for all believers. The church is supposed to be filled with people who have both power and the character to wield that power. The problem is for far too long we have been eating the scraps from Longshanks's table.

Christ came as a man to show us what is possible for human beings who are filled with the power of heaven. Healing the sick, raising the dead, and casting out demons were activities Christ accomplished here on earth. But he wasn't the only one doing these works—no, far from it. As we have already discovered, the twelve apostles did these great signs and so did at least another seventy-two. For that matter, so did the young New Testament church. The disciples expected that kind of power, even after Jesus left for home. That's because Jesus said he was going to give it to them: "You are witnesses of these things. And behold, I am sending the promise of my Father upon you. But stay in the city until you are clothed with power from on high" (Luke 24:48–49).

The early church received that kind of power, and for that matter, you can receive it too. How do you like them apples?

We distance ourselves from the New Testament church because we have embraced the lie that we are *not* the New Testament church. We have been told they were so much more pure and holy than we are. I hate that. It's a bunch of baloney, and whoever made that up stopped reading their Bible at Acts chapter 6. Just look at the Corinthian church. The main issue in that community was what to do with the guy who was having open sex with his step-mom and the church softball team who came to Sunday worship to get hammered on communion wine. I have some shocking news for you: we are better and more mature than the New Testament church. We have moved so far past their problems, it's ridiculous to even think about those things happening now. But, sadly, unlike the New Testament church, we have yet to fully embrace their power. And all that needs to change.

Think about it this way. If God's kingdom is advancing (and it is); if Christ is going to reign until all his enemies surrender (and he is); and if Christ is using the church to stamp out Satan (which he is), then doesn't it stand to reason he will continue to clothe his church with power until the day we conquer all evil and usher in the new heavens and the news earth?

The answer: yes!

Gary North says, "A renewed earth and a renewed heaven is the final payment by God the Father and to his Son and to those he has given to his Son. But prior to this, Christianity will reign victorious on the earth."[67]

So, enough of this trembling in the corner. Christ is the King, and he has given us great power. You should expect that power as the disciples did. It's overwhelming to think about what life will be like when the church truly steps into its power. The world will change, the gospel will reach the ends of the earth, and creation will be restored. I honestly believe that in Christ all of the answers to the world's problem will

---

67   North, *Liberating Planet Earth*, 146.

be solved. We simply need to tap into his spigot and drink freely of his power. With a church acting like the church is supposed to act, the world's hunger will disappear, water will become abundant, prosperity will reign, and rape and incest will become a thing of the past and from an age long forgotten.

The keys to executing this game plan are simple. First, we must remember we have authority. Then, we must back authority with power. We must then follow Christ's lead (and not Adam's) to use our dominion well, asking for more power through prayer, fasting, and obedience. Then, we must use that power to change the world.

It's possible and it can occur. Of course, the key to making this work is to do it all on God's timing and with his specific direction, the subject of which we will cover in the next section as we delve into the Gospel of John.

SECTION 5:

CHRIST THE MAN WHOSE TIME HAD COME

SECTION 5:
CHRIST THE MAN WHOSE TIME HAD COME

"For everything there is a season, and a time for every matter under heaven."

— Ecclesiastes 3:1

"When Jesus had spoken these words, he lifted up his eyes to heaven, and said, 'Father, the hour has come; glorify your Son that the Son may glorify you.'"

— John 17:1

HITLER WAS AN idiot.

One of history's most powerful leaders was also one of history's most unprepared leaders. Having risen only to corporal in World War I, Hitler never achieved a military rank that would have resulted in any actual leadership experience in the field. This fault eventually became his downfall. During the rise of the Third Reich, Hitler compounded his problems by becoming myopic. Unwilling to listen to reports coming from the field, he chose instead to listen to grandiose and falsified claims of speed and impending success. Behind his back, his most successful generals (men like Erwin Rommel) called him "the little corporal"—a jab at both his size and lack of military acumen.

But Hitler's biggest blunder was when he declared war on the United States.

On December 7, 1941, Japan made a surprise attack on the U.S. base at Pearl Harbor. Four days later, on December 11, Hitler declared war on the United States. It was the single decision that accelerated his demise.

Historian Michael Coffey puts it this way:

It was ironic that through his hasty step Hitler succeeded where Britain had so far failed in bringing America into the war. While the U.S. supply of arms to the Soviet Union and Britain and activities by the U.S. Navy in the North Atlantic demonstrated increasing American support for the Allied cause and were sources of irritation to Hitler, American isolationism prevented her from becoming actively involved in the European conflict. A Gallup poll in 1940 showed that 80 percent of Americans were against entering the war. It was Japan that persuaded Hitler to declare war on the United States. He hoped that Japan would do him a favor in return by moving against the Soviet Union. But he was wrong.[68]

Hitler was an untrained and unprepared man. And despite his rhetoric and military power, he was ultimately destined to fail. That's because when untrained men enter a war they are unprepared for, they always fail. What is true on the earthly plane is doubly true on the spiritual plane. When Christian men and women take up arms to fight a battle they are unprepared for, they will lose. It happens to well-meaning Christians every day.

It is an important point, and it is central to the book of John where the warrior theme is *timing*.

---

68   Michael Coffey, *Military Blunders* (New York, NY: Hyperion, 2000), 81.

Jesus waited thirty years to take the stage as the Jewish Messiah. And once he made himself publically known, he carefully weaved himself in and out of situations and conversations, working his three years for maximum effect. Then, and only when his time had fully come, was he ready for his greatest battle at the cross.

But before we look at the preparation of Christ and what it meant that his time had come, let's take a look at what occurs when untrained, unprepared Christians go to battle.

CHAPTER 17:

THE MAN WHOSE TIME HAD NOT COME

JOHN MAY HAVE been Jesus' favorite apostle, but if you ask the guys at church who their favorite apostle is, almost all of them will say Peter. That's because Peter is so much like...us. And we love him for it. He is a virtual roller coaster of good and bad. On a good day, Peter shines. On a bad day, he is an apt reminder we are all so human.

I've never met Peter (although I plan to someday). Nevertheless, I am pretty sure the motto on Peter's family crest reads: *Paratus Ignis Concupisco.* That's Latin for "Ready, FIRE, Aim." To put it bluntly, he was a guy who spoke first and asked questions later.

And so it should not surprise us that among all the mistakes in the Bible, Peter's denial of Christ took the prize at the county fair. The ribbon reads: Apostolic Blunder Number One.

We pick up the story at John 13. It was the night of the Last Supper, and all the boys (Peter included) thought the fight against Rome was going to start soon. They enjoyed quite a full meal of bread with wine, and Jesus finished washing their feet, which was uncomfortable at best. Jesus then told his friends he was going away for a while—three days in a tomb.

To say the apostles didn't grasp what he meant is an understatement. It wasn't Jesus' fault either. He did all he could do. They were just not prepared for a battle they were not called to fight in the first place. Let's listen in to the discussion at the Upper Room: "Simon Peter said to him, 'Lord, where are you going?' Jesus answered him, 'Where I am going you cannot follow me now, but you will follow afterward.' Peter said to him, 'Lord, why can I not follow you now? I will lay down my life for you.' Jesus answered, 'Will you lay down your life for me?'" (John 13:36–38).

Peter actually believed this. He was not pretending. But then again, having never seen real bullets fly, Peter had no idea what his promise meant. It is a military adage that the one who brags the most in peace is often the one who surrenders the fastest in war—that it's often the quiet, steady one who proves to be the best soldier. Peter, like the other apostles, was untrained, unprepared, and uncalled for this particular fight. The battle that night was Christ's alone.

I am convinced that had Peter asked Jesus for advice, he would have gotten it. The conversation probably would have gone like this:

> *Peter:* Jesus, can we talk for a minute? I know something big is going down tonight, and I am not sure I am ready for it. So, I would really like your advice. Knowing what you know about my character, what do you think I should do when the bullets start flying?

> *Jesus:* You basically have two options. If you really want to fight with me tonight, then start praying now. And don't stop praying until Sunday morning. The devil is coming, and you are going to need all the help you can get. If you can't devote yourself fully to prayer, then the moment you see the guards: RUN!

As you know, Peter did not ask for advice, nor did he ask for help. Instead, he blindly proclaimed his steadfast and undying devotion to his Master.

Jesus was unimpressed: "'Simon, Simon, behold, Satan demanded to have you, that he might sift you like wheat, but I have prayed for you that your faith may not fail. And when you have turned again, strengthen your brothers.' Peter said to him, 'Lord, I am ready to go with you both to prison and to death.' Jesus said, 'I tell you, Peter, the rooster will not crow this day, until you deny three times that you know me'" (Luke 22:31–34).

Jesus, in effect, said Peter was going down. Satan asked to drop him to his knees, and God was going to allow it to occur. Peter's steadfast refusal to listen to Christ's warning only magnified his failure.

You know the rest of the story. Jesus prayed in the garden while Peter took a nap on his sword. The action heated up when the temple soldiers came to arrest Jesus.

> While he was still speaking, there came a crowd, and the man called Judas, one of the twelve, was leading them. He drew near to Jesus to kiss him, but Jesus said to him, "Judas, would you betray the Son of Man with a kiss?" And when those who were around him saw what would follow, they said, "Lord, shall we strike with the sword?" And one of them [Peter] struck the servant of the high priest and cut off his right ear. But Jesus said, "No more of this!" And he touched his ear and healed him. (Luke 22:47–50)

You really do have to hand it to Peter. At least he came out of the corner swinging. His first move was as foolish as it was brave. In typical Peter style, he didn't even wait for an answer to his question. He swung his sword while asking to swing his sword.

Apparently, although Peter was quite good at tending to fishnets, he wasn't very skilled with a weapon. He missed the servant's head (by a lot) and barely cut off a small bit of his ear.

Not exactly William Wallace.

Then, instead of running away like the rest of the gang, Peter decided to stick around and follow a safe distance behind. Here is where the mistakes started to pile up. Three somewhat insignificant people, each in succession, asked Peter whether he knew Jesus. The Bible describes his answers as pathetic. At one point, he actually started to spit and curse at himself, swearing under oath that he *never* knew Jesus...ever: "And again he denied it with an oath: 'I do not know the man.' After a little while the bystanders came up and said to Peter, 'Certainly you too are one of them, for your accent betrays you.' Then he began to invoke a curse on himself and to swear, 'I do not know the man.' And immediately the rooster crowed" (Matthew 26:72–74).

Peter basically lied, "I never knew Jesus and I never will. I'm just here to get warm like the rest of you!"

It has been said Christians fight against three things: the world, the flesh, and the devil. Peter battled all three on that fateful night. And together, they joined forces to beat him senseless.

The *world* set the stage. A crowd of people came to see Jesus arrested. They were the modern-day version of rubberneckers, those folks who slow down to see the accident on the side of the road. All the "world" did that night was stand by the fire and tell Peter he was with Christ, which, of course, he was.

The *flesh* was clearly evident in Peter's personal pride. He really did believe he was invincible, even to the point he passed on Jesus' advice to pray and took a nap instead. Peter's fall was so predictable Christ nailed it even to the hour, to sunrise. "Peter, you won't even make it until dawn."

Finally, there is the *devil*—he was the one who actually tempted Peter (although Peter walked right through the door just fine on his own). But before we get too harsh on Peter, just imagine being tempted by the prince of darkness. Not many men could stand up to that—especially men whose motto is "Ready, fire, aim."

Seriously, think of your biggest sin issue, then multiply that temptation by about a hundred times. Then, totally disregard what Jesus says, then see what happens. No one, and I mean no one, could have endured that night's temptation save Christ himself. He was the only one prepared for a fight. And he was the only one called to fight that night.

So the point becomes crystal clear. As soldiers, we are meant to fight only those battles we have been called to fight. And once we start fighting, we must expect to fight the world (your environment), the flesh (your indwelling sin), and the devil (the tempter and accuser). The applications of this point could be endless.

For example, what is your biggest sin issue? Pride, gossip, lust, anger? The list goes on and on. Whatever it is, the very first thing you can do to battle your sin is to simply avoid the occasions where you are most tempted (i.e., the environment).

Here is one of mine. I tend to get angry with my kids right before a meal. Five minutes before dinner last night, I told my kids to wash their hands, get a glass of water, and meet me at the table. Five minutes later, they hadn't even washed their hands. That drives me nuts. Given that situation, I usually raise my voice and monologue about how I am in charge, how they must listen, how they must obey, how hard I work, and on and on and on. It's ridiculous. Picture Hitler in one of his famous speeches.

It feels totally justified, but it's totally sin.

What's really happening in this scenario? Three words: I am hungry. Three more words: I am selfish. The world set the stage, my flesh prepared the ground, and the devil closed the deal.

So, if I really wanted to win this battle, I wouldn't even go there. Instead, I would literally take myself out of the environment of temptation. In this instance, I would eat some fruit to curb my hunger and then just mentally agree that cold food is preferable to an angry dad. That's what I mean when I say some battles are not meant to be fought. Some battles are meant to be avoided.

The same could be true for almost every battle you frequently lose. Take for example, pornography.

Did he just go there?

Oh, yes I did.

I have a friend who, upon checking into his hotel room, literally calls the front desk and asks them to remove the TV. He doesn't only unplug it. He has it *removed* entirely. So, if you have an issue with on-demand movies, get a couple of hotel staff to remove the TV. Just tell them you are Muslim or something and that it's against your religion. They will take the TV out, and you will have one less battle to fight. Then, go get some healing and some training so someday you can safely have a TV in your room again.

The examples, however, are not restricted only to sin issues. We talked back in chapter 7 about how to get serious about your mission. Needless to say, some perfectly good missions are not yours to fight. It's not your job to save everyone you meet. It's not your job to minister to everyone in need. And it's not your job to volunteer for every job in the church. That's the kind of thing that creates a great deal of pride and also creates a lot of empty chairs at the family dinner table.

The key, of course, is to ask Jesus for his specific direction about the battles you are facing: which ones to fight and which ones to leave for someone else to fight. Peter's biggest mistake was he was so puffed up with his own pride it never even occurred to him to ask Jesus for direction. It's our biggest mistake too.

So, now that we have seen precisely what not to do, let's take a look at the Man who fought the missions he was called to fight and how he did it.

CHAPTER 18:
STRENGTH IN WAITING

I AM PRETTY SURE civil engineers receive their diplomas along with a free McDonald's Happy Meal. I'm serious. For some reason, the city of San Diego (where I live) has fallen in love with left-hand turning lights (those are the ones with the arrow). Now, I get it. Some intersections are so busy you could never turn left without a left-hand light. But a bunch of intersections near me barely have enough traffic for a stop sign, much less a left-hand turning arrow.

So, there I sit with my blinker on...click...click...click. There's no one coming in the other direction...click...click... click. And no one ever will...click...click...click. So there I sit at the light waiting...click...click...click...and waiting...click...click... click...and waiting.

Frankly, that drives me crazy. Just ask my wife. *I hate waiting.*

So you can imagine how frustrating it was a year ago when I asked God for my life's mission and he said, "Wait." I'll tell you that story in a minute, but first let's jump back into the book of John.

There is a seemingly out-of-place line in the midst of Jesus' first miracle, the wedding at Cana. Do you remember the story? The bride and groom were halfway through the reception, and the wine ran out. That was a major party foul, and there would be hell to pay if this didn't get fixed—and fast. But that was first-century Palestine and not twenty-first-century Chicago. Back then, if you wanted more wine, you couldn't run down to the Quickie Mart for a few bottles of Kendall Jackson. You had to... well, start with the grapes...wait for a year...ferment the grapes... and wait another year. You get the picture.

Jesus was both kind and generous, so when Mary asked him to help, he mixed up a batch of wine so good the guests went wild and the party raged on until the wee hours of the morning. Jesus made the equivalent of somewhere between

600 and 950 bottles of wine, which is also awesome. Jesus was a great guy to have at a party.[69]

Listen to the story from John's vantage point: "On the third day there was a wedding at Cana in Galilee, and the mother of Jesus was there. Jesus also was invited to the wedding with his disciples. When the wine ran out, the mother of Jesus said to him, 'They have no wine.' And Jesus said to her, 'Woman, what does this have to do with me? My hour has not yet come.' His mother said to the servants, 'Do whatever he tells you'" (John 2:1–5).

That one line, "My hour has not yet come," has had Bible commentators in a bind ever since Jesus said it. Some say Jesus never actually intended to do a miracle, but that Mary talked him into it. Others say Jesus was speaking of his death and resurrection. Others say he didn't want to attract too much attention so early on in his career.

Honestly, I am not sure who is right, and I don't think it really matters. What does matter is Jesus had obviously been telling himself this very thing for quite a long time.

My time has not yet come.

Picture this. Since Jesus was at least twelve years old, he was fully aware he was the Son of God. And because he knew

---

69   Thank you to John Eldredge for reminding God's people that Jesus was a lot of fun. For example, if you can't imagine Jesus drinking a glass of wine and telling a good joke, then you aren't imagining the *real* Jesus. It's time to fix that, like ASAP. Read Eldredge's book *Beautiful Outlaw*. While you are at it, read the Gospels too. Then stop and imagine yourself in the story. Stay there for a while. If you are like me, you'll probably see Jesus smile and your world will change.

he was God, he also knew he could make bread, heal the sick, raise the dead, walk on water, and read people's minds. It was a lot for a twelve-year-old, but then again he wasn't your average twelve-year-old.

Luke tells us this: "After three days they found him in the temple, sitting among the teachers, listening to them and asking them questions. And all who heard him were amazed at his understanding and his answers" (Luke 2:46–47).

His spiritual understanding at age twelve was, in a word, *astounding.*

Yet, for eighteen more years, Jesus apparently did… nothing. According to every record we have, it seems Jesus simply submitted himself to his earthly father and lived his life as a normal carpenter. He built homes, made tables, and carried lumber. During that time, while fully knowing he was God, he simply hammered, sawed, planed, and sanded.

Just imagine a few possible scenarios.

Picture Jesus slicing his hand on a nail. As he wrapped it with a bandage, his mind flashed forward to another nail—a nail that would do more than just open a wound; it would go right through his hand. Just then, in the carpenter shop, Jesus whispered under his breath, "My time has not yet come."

Later that week, Jesus may have heard a scream as he walked by the home of his Aunt Eliana. She's had trouble breathing for weeks, but now it seems, she could hardly get a breath in or out. In his mind's eye, Jesus saw his aunt suffering from acute emphysema. He also knew with only a word he could give her brand-new lungs, without which she's dead in five minutes. Jesus didn't heal her, nor did he raise her from the dead.

He did...nothing. And as he left the home, he whispered under his breath, "My time has not yet come."

On his sixteenth birthday, Jesus' parents may have taken him to Jerusalem for a visit to the temple. What he saw there was, in a word, *appalling*. Jewish leaders with their jingling robes commanded the glory of the crowd—they purposely made their faces look gloomy during a fast, just for an extra round of applause. The marketplace was a zoo, and Jesus saw an ox cart run over a leper. Six Pharisees also saw it happen, but they quickly returned to their argument about the weight of the temple's gold. They would have helped the man, of course, but then again, he was a leper—and the feast was that afternoon. Welling up inside Jesus was a mixture of anger, compassion, and fear. He could cleanse the temple right there. He could heal the leper and rebuke the Pharisees. He *wanted* to. He *yearned* to.

And yet, he did...nothing. As Jesus left Jerusalem, he whispered under his breath, "My time has not yet come."

Jesus witnessed every kind of tragedy known to man. He saw the boat sink in the Galilean storm sending ten men to the bottom. He saw a blind man ridiculed on the street. He saw the child abandoned by his parents. He saw the sickness, the shame, the abuse, and the neglect, and yet, even up until that very moment in Cana, every time he was tempted to act, he did...nothing. He simply whispered under his breath, "My time has not yet come."

Jesus waited because he knew his three years in public ministry would take all the strength and preparation he could muster. So he kept his strength in check to prepare for the day he would launch onto the scene and change the world. Had he chosen to act in any of the (imagined) scenarios above or any of the real ones just like them, he would have called undo attention to himself way before his time. In short, his real mission was far too risky to enter the battle too young or unprepared.

And so Jesus waited.

And sometimes, we must wait too.

Let me tell you about a time God told me to wait.

Have you ever had one of those seasons where you keep coming back to a verse in the Bible and you have no idea why? That happened to me one year ago. For almost two months, my Bible seemed to always open directly to this passage in Isaiah:

> Even youths shall faint and be weary,
>
> and young men shall fall exhausted;
>
> but they who wait for the LORD shall renew their strength;
>
> they shall mount up with wings like eagles;
>
> they shall run and not be weary;
>
> they shall walk and not faint. (Isaiah 40:30–31)

This happened so frequently I finally threw my hands up and said, "OK, God, I have no idea why you keep showing me this passage, but if you are trying to tell me something, please let me know what it is."

My main focus during that time was finding my true mission in life. I knew God placed me on this earth for a reason. I knew I was given certain gifts. And I wanted God to give me my orders.

It was right in the midst of that struggle when I had a phone conversation with author and speaker Gary Barkalow. Gary wrote the book *It's Your Call*, and he's particularly gifted at helping men find their place in the Kingdom.

The first forty-five minutes of the discussion were frustrating for both of us. Gary was asking great questions, and, honestly, I didn't have any answers. We were both trying, but it was as if we were hitting a stone wall. Finally, Gary (wisely) said, "You know, Ed, sometimes we sit here and try to figure things out while the whole time God has something to say. Let's just pray and ask him if he has anything he wants to say to you."

So we closed our eyes and prayed that God would speak. Then, we were silent for about four minutes.

After the silence, Gary asked me, "So, did you hear anything from God?"

"Nope."

He said, "Well, I feel like he gave me an impression. Do you mind if I share it with you?"

Gary went on to tell a story about the navigation computers on a jumbo jet. You see, when any jet stops at the gate, the pilot has to shut down the navigation system, and then restart it. During those first few minutes, the plane must remain absolutely still. That's because all the navigation gyros need to be aligned perfectly before the pilot can download the new maps.

The moral is: the plane needs to be still before getting its new instructions.

That hit me like a ton of bricks.

You see, I have always been a busy, driven, and purposeful man. For thirteen years, I was a fighter pilot in the Marine Corps. I went on four deployments overseas (two to Iraq and two to Japan). And at the height of my career, I was the number one instructor in the entire Marine Corps for several weapons systems.

As soon as I left the Marine Corps, I simultaneously started an online business and a speaking business. Then I started a consulting business. Then I started a service business.

Then, the wheels started falling off the cart.

Quite the opposite to Isaiah 40, I ran and grew weary. I walked and grew faint. That's because in many ways, I was running for me. By last year, my tank was empty and my strength was gone.

What God told me through Isaiah 40 and through wise council became perfectly apparent: my mission was to wait on God and renew my strength. The reason, God said was so "the next time, you can run and *not* grow weary."

A week later, I went camping. On Sunday morning, one of the guys led a devotion around the fire. Guess what passage he talked about? Yup, Isaiah 40, waiting on the Lord. (When God wants to make a point, he makes his point!)

So I obediently waited to renew my strength. I dropped the question of my calling all together and walked with the Lord. I simply asked God to resurrect the issue of calling when he wanted to bring it back.

This book is what he brought back.

Friend, there is strength in waiting. As you follow Christ into battle, you must remember to fight only the battles he has called you to and only when you are prepared. In the times where he is not calling you to fight, he is calling you to wait. Christ waited for at least eighteen years...and he was God. If he needed to wait to renew his strength, it stands to reason from time to time you do too.

Of course, there are times to wait and there are times to fight. And only God (and your training) can tell you which is which. So, let's look at how Christ chose his battles so we can know how to choose ours.

CHAPTER 19:
WHEN YOUR TIME COMES

HERE IS A recent spoof "news" story on the importance of being prepared:

Police in the West Midlands have today arrested a Scoutmaster who, in direct contravention of the ancient rules laid down by Lord Baden-Powell, took some Boy Scouts out on a camping trip "totally unprepared."

"Tatty" Mullett, 24, was in charge of a group of Scouts from the Royal 116th Bearwood Mounted Hussars Troop when they set out upon a camping weekend in Shropshire. On arrival at the camp site, it was decided the group should "chow down" with a pre-packed picnic the Scoutmaster prepared.

It was only then the hungry little blighters discovered their leader had broken the first rule of Scouting—Be Prepared—and left the grub at home.

When Police raided Mullett's home in Birmingham, they found a scene of "absolute devastation, " every room being in a state of "complete unpreparedness." Detective Chief Superintendent Ben Clarinet of West Midlands police, told reporters:

"The place was in total disarray. There were neckerchiefs and toggles everywhere."

Mr. Mullett, who is also a spare-time computer geek, was charged under Section 4a of the Anti-forgetfulness Act, and was placed in the custody of his mom.

Alan Notready, of the Crown Prosecution Service, said: "He should be prepared to go away for a long time."[70]

It's a joke, but it fits, doesn't it?

All too often the church launches its members into battles they are not prepared for...and we reap the consequences.

We send a missionary overseas and into the heart of China when he is too young in the faith. He tries, fails, and then comes home with a loss of heart so great he will never recover.

---

70   http://www.thespoof.com/news/spoof.cfm?headline=s1i17610

We ask the mother of three to lead the children's program. She has a hard enough time keeping her own kids in check, much less twenty others. She resigns and swears to never work with church kids again.

We recognize "ministry gifts" in a young man in our church—basically he is a good speaker and he loves Jesus. So we send him off to seminary where instead of doing ministry he learns about ministry. Instead of knowing God, he learns to know about God.[71] Because he is too young, he is changed forever. And he will never fight a single meaningful battle for the rest of his life.

Jesus, on the other hand, hit his thirtieth year and walked onto the scene with everything he needed to win his battles. He had the experience; he had the power; and most of all, he had a deep and abiding relationship with his Father.

What's more, he had total and complete control of every situation. For example, several times in the Bible, Jesus seemed

---

71 There are a lot of good seminaries doing *good* work, and I deeply appreciate the good and godly men (and women) who teach at seminaries. Having said that, I have a fundamental issue with the idea of taking a warrior out of the battle so he can learn about the battle. That's not what Jesus did. Nor is it what he does now. I have known many young seminary graduates—I even mentored a few. With precious few exceptions, I discovered most were trained how to argue well for the Kingdom but not how to fight well for the Kingdom. No wonder entire denominations spend their every waking minute fighting each other. It's what they were trained to do in the first place. A solution to this problem is to keep the training of pastors at the local level. Teach them to serve while they are serving. We have one such example here in San Diego at Harbor Presbyterian Church. It is commendable.

to just slip out of the hands of the religious leaders or the people. Here are a few of those times:

> They said to him therefore, "Where is your Father?" Jesus answered, "You know neither me nor my Father. If you knew me, you would know my Father also." These words he spoke in the treasury, as he taught in the temple; but no one arrested him, because his hour had not yet come. (John 8:19–20)
>
> When they heard these things, all in the synagogue were filled with wrath. And they rose up and drove him out of the town and brought him to the brow of the hill on which their town was built, so that they could throw him down the cliff. But passing through their midst, he went away. (Luke 4:28–30)
>
> Perceiving then that they were about to come and take him by force to make him king, Jesus withdrew again to the mountain by himself. (John 6:15)
>
> Jesus said to them, "Truly, truly, I say to you, before Abraham was, I am." So they picked up stones to throw at him, but Jesus hid himself and went out of the temple. (John 8:58–59)
>
> The Pharisees heard the crowd muttering these things about him, and the chief priests and Pharisees sent officers to arrest him. (John 7:32)

Jesus' teaching always evoked one of two reactions: either the people tried to make him king or the leaders tried to kill him. These scenes occurred all too often for them to be coincidental, one-time acts.

It's crazy.

Just look at that last passage. John tells us the Pharisees sent officers to arrest Jesus. That was in John 7, long before Jesus went to the cross. What happened to that arrest warrant? For that matter, what happened to the officers? John doesn't even give us the courtesy of knowing how that story finishes. Clearly, they didn't end up arresting Jesus because he was in the temple teaching the very next day.

Earlier, Jesus literally just walked through a crowd that intended to throw him off a cliff. He didn't even say a word. They went to the edge of the cliff to toss him off, and he virtually ignored them. Again, there was no explanation, no pleading, and no speech. Jesus didn't even run—he walked.

I honestly think the reason the crowd let Jesus walk by was they were simply shocked by his apparent lack of a reaction. Think about it. What do people normally do before they are about to be thrown off a cliff?

They plead, beg, and scream for their lives.

What did Jesus do? He just walked calmly through the crowd. Remarkable.

Here was a man in total control of every situation. His control came from three things: first, he was trained; second, he was prepared; and third, he walked daily with the Father. Sure, he was God, and that must have factored into it. But then again, the life of Christ was intended to show us what a true human could accomplish, and so, as unbelievable as it seems, this kind of control can be possible for you too.

Christ's situational control meant nothing, and I mean nothing could happen to him that he didn't first allow. That also meant when he rode into Jerusalem at the beginning of that final Passover week, he knew exactly where he is going. For the first time in thirty-three years, Jesus stretched out his hands and allowed the very people he created to jam thorns in his head, nails in his hands, and a spear in his side. He did so willingly and Paul tells us why: "For while we were still weak, at the right time Christ died for the ungodly. For one will scarcely die for a righteous person—though perhaps for a good person one would dare even to die—but God shows his love for us in that while we were still sinners, Christ died for us" (Romans 5:6–8).

For at least 4,000 years, God waited to save his people. Finally, it was time to act. Paul says he did it because it was the right time.

Jesus came as a chosen warrior. He came as a King. He came as a valiant leader. And he came as a servant.

He came because his time had come, and he said, "Behold, the hour is coming, indeed it has come, when you will be scattered, each to his own home, and will leave me alone. Yet I am not alone, for the Father is with me. I have said these things to you, that in me you may have peace. In the world you will have tribulation. But take heart; I have overcome the world" (John 16:32–33).

Jesus waited patiently. But once he got the green light, he moved fast and he moved decisively to claim the victory that was his (and yours). The warrior principle is simply this: when a warrior is called to move, he moves.

All the preparation and all the waiting come down to the decisive moment of battle. Our spiritual weapons include words, prayer, action, deliverance, healing, blessing, or simply comforting. The keys to success are threefold. First, you must prepare for the battle. Second, you must wait for the right time. Third, you must fight.

When, like Christ, you combine these three keys, you will win,...

and the world will never be the same again.

Oh, and let's not forget about Peter. History tells us he served Christ faithfully into old age, and like his Master, he also was crucified. According to tradition, Peter asked to hang upside down on the cross as he deemed himself unworthy to die as Jesus died.

Unlike his previous bout with the devil, Peter was prepared for this battle. He waited for the right time. He fought willingly for Christ. And in a story only God could write, Peter finally fulfilled his promise to lay down his life for his friend.

We see then there are times when a warrior must fight and there are times when he must simply endure. That will be the subject of our next section.

SECTION 6:

CHRIST THE MAN
WHO ENDURED

Section 6:
Christ the Man Who Endured

"Joseph suffered thirteen years of hardship, loss, persecution, and abandonment. But God understood the pressures that Joseph's character needed to withstand in order to succeed once he was promoted to rule over Egypt....Joseph's soul and character had to be purified and strengthened through these tests in managing what was another's. Otherwise, he would not have had the capacity and wisdom to stand in the place of authority and power to manage the wealth of a vast nation such as Egypt."[72]

— Steven DeSilva

"Endure suffering along with me, as a good soldier of Christ Jesus."

— 2 Timothy 2:3 NLT

---

72   Steven DeSilva, *Money and the Prosperous Soul* (St. Royal Oak, MI: Chosen Books, 2010), 48.

D O YOU WANT to know the number one lie in the airline industry? I will give you a hint. It's not gas prices, arrival times, or where your luggage ended up. It's not why its twenty-five dollars to check a bag or fifty dollars for "more legroom."

The biggest lie in the airline industry has gone completely unnoticed, but I'll bet you've heard it a thousand times.

Here it goes: *At Delta, Safety Is Our Number #1 Priority.*

It's total baloney. And here's why. If safety were actually their number one priority, then why in heaven's name are they shoving 220 of us into a steel tube, surrounded by gas and oil, then light a match on the ignition and fly up to 36,000 feet and 500 miles per hour?

That doesn't sound safe, does it?

If I had to bet, safety would probably come around number three or four on the priority list. First would be mission accomplishment—getting you there. Second would be profit. Third would be customer satisfaction. Then safety, fourth.

I would pay money to hear this broadcasted over the loud speaker of a Boeing 737: "[Unnaturally deep and raspy voice] Ahhhhh...Hello, ladies and gentleman, I am Captain Mumble-Mouth, and this is First Officer Lands-Too-Hard. We want to welcome you to flight 342 with nonstop service to Atlanta. And as a reminder, here at Delta, Safety is probably our third or fourth concern. Seriously, it's way down the list. So buckle in and enjoy your short flight."

To be fair, airlines are not the only ones who fake it when it comes to their missions. Have you seen any military recruiting commercials lately? Think about this. The military wants recruits to donate their time (and maybe their lives) to the cause of freedom. They want them to spend several years in a foxhole or in Afghanistan, or both. And they want them to be away from their families for six to nine months at a time.

Here is how they do it.

"Be all that you can be!"

"Get an edge on life!"

"It's a great place to start!"

"It's not just a job. It's an adventure!"

(As an aside, this last one is particularly insidious. That's because it's from the Navy. It should actually sound like this: "Come float on the ocean alone for nine months, get seasick, and paint our ships for eight hours a day!")

I am thankful the Marine Corps has pretty much stuck to their guns:

"The Few. The Proud. The Marines."

"Earned. Never Given."

(I am so biased.)

Just like Delta, the military cloaks the real issue. Real battles are fought with real guns and real bullets. People really shoot at you, and people really die. It occurs every day, and you better get used to it because in the military safety isn't anywhere close to the number one priority.

The good news is, unlike the airlines or the military, God is 100 percent unambiguous when it comes to his warrior recruiting slogans. His reads like this: "Endure suffering along with me, as a good soldier of Christ Jesus" (2 Timothy 2:3 NLT).

That's it. No money for college. No G.I. Bill. The call of a Christian warrior involves suffering, and there is nothing you can do about it. Yet every single day, brave men and women enlist in Christ's army, and many lose their lives in the fight. Why? What could possibly be so appealing that literally millions have answered this call?

Well, the answer is twofold: Christ is the best Commander to fight for, and this war is the only place where you are guaranteed a win.

Even though the battle is fierce and lives are at risk, we know we have, as Hebrews tells us, "a great high priest who has passed through the heavens, Jesus, the Son of God" (Hebrews 4:14). He has endured and he has prevailed. And so when it comes right down to it, nothing can beat us. We will win. That is a given. And so the only thing the enemy can really do is harass and slow us down.

Paul confidently tells us we will win, even in the midst of suffering: "No, in all these things we are more than conquerors through him who loved us. For I am sure that neither death nor life, nor angels nor rulers, nor things present nor things to come, nor powers, nor height nor depth, nor anything else in all creation, will be able to separate us from the love of God in Christ Jesus our Lord" (Romans 8:37–39).

In the meantime, the recruiting slogan still holds true. If you are going to serve the cause of Christ, you are going to suffer. I hate to put it that way, but the Bible treats suffering as a fact of life. It is going to occur whether you like it or not. In fact, it's actually a part of your training.

But whatever you do, do not skip this section (I know it's tempting). After all, who wants to talk about pain and misery? Heck, I didn't even want to write this section because to ethically write about something means you need to have lived it.

Even though I am going to be talking about a somewhat negative subject, believe-you-me it has quite a happy ending. That's because Christian suffering is not permanent. Suffering is never, and I mean never, supposed to be an unending state for a Christian. It is a temporary means to a permanent end. Now I know at times suffering may feel permanent. But sooner or later, in this life or in the next, you will get your breakthrough. You will get your victory. And as the Kingdom comes on earth as it is in heaven, the breakthroughs will come more here on earth than in heaven too.

That is really good news.

So now that you know Christ's recruiting slogan and now that you have enlisted in Christ's army, let's together learn more about suffering so we can get past it and onto victory.

As usual, we will look at the life of Christ as our example in battle. Having unpacked the warrior themes in all four Gospels, we now turn our attention to the one event all four Gospels highlight as the great climax of their respective stories: the death of Christ.

When we look at the suffering of Christ, we see there are several keys for enduring suffering as a good soldier.

CHAPTER 20:
CONTROL WHAT YOU CAN CONTROL

JESUS' COMPOSURE UNDER stress was breathtaking. He was whipped, beaten, harassed, ridiculed, nailed to a cross, and left for hours to either bleed or suffocate to death. Through it all, he didn't miss one word and he never got upset. Jesus endured his suffering for the most part, silently. Compare his composure to that of his enemies. They endured no suffering, yet they made absolute fools of themselves.

To really understand the surprising self-control of the Suffering Servant, you must first use your imagination and place yourself in the story. Far too often, our Bible reading is quick and cursory, and by virtue of that, we fail to grasp the details. Think of it this way. When we read our Bibles like a trip through the multiplex movie theater, spending five minutes in each movie, we shouldn't be surprised when we don't know the details. So, for a moment, let's use our imagination and experience Christ's suffering from his point of view.

This first vignette comes from Luke: "Now the men who were holding Jesus in custody were mocking him as they beat him. They also blindfolded him and kept asking him, 'Prophesy! Who is it that struck you?' And they said many other things against him, blaspheming him" (Luke 22:63–65).

Now, take a moment to absorb this: the men punched God in the face, and he did...nothing. Seriously, have you ever been punched in the face? I have. Do you know what happens when you get punched in the face? You go wild. I am not kidding. The second that jab lands on your chin, emotion takes over and you become a crazed lunatic. Our very instincts demand us to react like that—it's that whole fight-or-flight thing.

Now imagine for a moment you are the Son of God. The temple guard blindfolds you and starts pounding on your face. You feel your nose break and blood drip down your throat. In your all-knowing mind, you go back twenty years to see the guard as a child. You witness him stealing money from his mom's purse. Then you fast forward to this afternoon where you earlier had seen him looking lustfully at the local Jerusalem wench.

Wouldn't it be tempting to drop those two tasty tidbits on him?

Hit me again, Johnny Lebowitz, and I'll tell your mom you stole her money, and I'll tell your wife you're in love with the town whore.

It would be so good.

And yet Jesus kept his mouth completely shut.

Here is another scene—this one from Mark. Again, place yourself in the story:

> Now the chief priests and the whole council were seeking testimony against Jesus to put him to death, but they found none. For many bore false witness against him, but their testimony did not agree. And some stood up and bore false witness against him, saying, "We heard him say, 'I will destroy this temple that is made with hands, and in three days I will build another, not made with hands.'" Yet even about this their testimony did not agree. (Mark 14:55–59)

The scene is ridiculous. By Jewish law, at least two witnesses were required to deliver flawless accounts in order for a defendant to be rightfully prosecuted. Instead, the Jewish leaders invented this entire story. And even though they practiced their lines over and over again, the witnesses still got it wrong. No one could agree on what happened in their little made-up accounts.

Imagine once again you are Jesus. In your mind's eye, you witness the meeting three weeks ago where the Jewish leaders paid two village idiots ten shekels apiece for their made-up story. Wouldn't it be tempting to jump in and say,

Hey, Yusef, I hope that ten shekel Happy Meal was worth it. You still can't seem to get this story right. Maybe you should have paid closer attention in Mrs. Rosenberg's ninth grade Hebrew class!

That alone would have dropped them to their knees. And yet Jesus kept his mouth completely shut. That's because Jesus understood his place in the battle. He knew, at least for the next twenty-four hours, vengeance was decidedly not his. He knew he could only control what he could control—namely his reaction to the situation.

The same is true for you and me.

You see, just like Christ's, your suffering often comes at the hands of evil men. Here are a few examples of real-life events I have either seen or heard.

Your boss constantly talks bad about you behind your back. So far, she has purposefully sidetracked two raises. That's because she doesn't like you. First, you are a threat to her job because you are better at it than she is. Second, you are a Christian. And she hates Christians. You have the goods on her, and you know you could take it to the head office. You choose, instead, to forgive her (and to keep forgiving her). You choose to give it to God. And you choose to let it go.

Your co-worker suddenly turns against you. He used to be your ally and now he hates your guts. To make matters worse, he owes you more than three thousand dollars. You know you could take him to court and win. You also know you could easily smear his public reputation. Both of those would be perfectly justified. You choose, instead, to forgive him (and to keep forgiving him). You choose to give it to God. And you choose to let it go.

Your mother-in-law always has you on pins and needles. Every time she comes to visit, she takes every opportunity to compare you to your in-laws. She offers a steady stream of unwelcome and unhelpful suggestions about the way you raise her grandkids. Worse, you know for a fact she talks bad about your parenting decisions to the other members of the family. Basically, you want to pop her in the eye. Instead, you choose to see her as a broken woman in need of the love of Christ. So for her, you become the love of Christ. It is done with much difficulty, but you love her nonetheless. You choose to forgive her (and to keep forgiving her). You choose to give it to God. And you choose (for the hundredth time) to let it go.

Incidentally, the same kind of betrayal happened to just about all the famous Bible characters. Here are a couple of examples.

Jacob's uncle Laban tried to cheat him out of about everything he rightfully earned. He even switched wives on Jacob just before the wedding vows. (Now that was *cold*.)

Joseph's brothers planned to kill him, but instead they made a few bucks by selling him as a slave. Potiphar's wife planned on having sex with him but instead had him thrown in jail on trumped-up charges. The king's cupbearer planned on helping Joseph get out of jail, but instead he forgot and enjoyed another drink with Pharaoh.

And David, well, you know his story. He planned on being king. Heck, he even slayed a giant when most adolescents were home playing *Angry Birds*. Instead, David spent much of his young life running, ducking, and hiding in caves to keep from being killed by Saul.

Like Christ, they did not entrust themselves to man. They simply kept their eyes on the goal and stayed close to the Father who promised, "If when you do good and suffer for it you endure, this is a gracious thing in the sight of God" (1 Peter 2:20).

Sure, at times you must fight. At times you should speak out against your boss, confront your mother-in-law, and take someone to court. But more times than not, the victory that comes through suffering is a victory best endured silently.

Know this, as long you endure as God would have you endure, you will win in the end. God will come through, and when he does, it will be awesome.

Just look at history.

Jacob became one of the richest men on earth and the father of nations. Joseph became second in command of all of Egypt and saved an entire generation of Israelites. David became king.

And Jesus won "an inheritance of nations."

But before any of that occurred, they all simply controlled what they could control—their reaction to their situation.

Similarly, when you are going through suffering, the first thing you must do is to simply control your reaction to the situation. More times than not, your best reaction will be total silence. You simply turn it all over to God and let him do the rest. In the midst of the whirlwind of sickness, loss, financial strain, and broken relationships, this is often the only thing you can control. And this is the first step toward victory.

The second step is to reject the enemy's lies and fight through the silence of God.

CHAPTER 21:
THE ENEMY'S LIES AND GOD'S SILENCE

FACE IT, YOU are not perfect. And this is where suffering can get sticky. We know Jesus' suffering was undeserved. We know he was perfect, sinless, and spotless. And we know immediately he was right, and they were wrong.

Our suffering, however, is not so clear-cut.

That's because deep down inside we know we are sinners, and because of that, there is a part of us that secretly thinks we deserve to suffer. But don't you believe that for a minute. One of the chief tactics the devil uses to keep us from breakthrough is to whisper in our ears that suffering is the result of our sin—and we deserve what is coming to us.

It's a lie.

The truth is you are indeed a sinner. But the cross of Christ canceled all that along with any claim the devil has on you. Listen carefully to what Paul says: "And you, who were dead in your trespasses and the uncircumcision of your flesh, God made alive together with him, having forgiven us all our trespasses, by canceling the record of debt that stood against us with its legal demands. This he set aside, nailing it to the cross. He disarmed the rulers and authorities and put them to open shame, by triumphing over them in him" (Colossians 2:13–15).

Paul makes this point quite clear: the devil has no claim on you. When you come to Christ, he forgives you, and when he does, any claim the evil one has over you is officially broken and disarmed. Your sin has been canceled. It was nailed to the cross 2,000 years ago, and God has forgotten it completely. It is totally true, even as much as it is totally hard to believe. That's why it is helpful to claim your freedom out loud.

When you are tempted to blame yourself for your suffering, say this: "I have been set free by the cross and the resurrection of Christ. Any claim against me has been canceled, broken, and disarmed."[73]

---

73   There is a very helpful "Daily Prayer" that has a longer version of this line. It is available at: http://www.ransomedheart.com/sites/default/files/assets/prayers/daily_prayer_script.pdf (or just search for "Ransomed Heart Daily Prayer").

Say it over and over again. Say it today, tonight, and tomorrow morning. Say it until you believe it. That is precisely because, at first, you will instinctively refuse to believe it. Then, you will start to get a glimmer of hope. Eventually it will stick. And that's when the enemy will flee. He will run because you displaced him with something greater. In other words, you have gained the ground.

Another lie the enemy whispers into your ear is that God is a long way off, and, to be clear, he is not all that interested in your petty little problems. We readily believe this lie based on the clear fact that, first, we have been praying, and second, we have not had an answer to our prayer. This lie is particularly insidious because it carefully matches all of the evidence. When you are tempted to believe that God is far off, go right to His Word and grab a hold of it like a life raft.

Try praying the Psalms—they are so honest. For example, read the end of Psalm 44.

> Awake! Why are you sleeping, O Lord?
>
> Rouse yourself! Do not reject us forever!
>
> Why do you hide your face?
>
> Why do you forget our affliction and oppression?
>
> For our soul is bowed down to the dust;
>
> our belly clings to the ground.
>
> Rise up; come to our help!
>
> Redeem us for the sake of your steadfast love!
>
> (Psalm 44:23–26)

Let's put this Psalm into a modern context to see how different Bible-praying is from our praying. Imagine you are at church this next Sunday morning. You've just finished singing all four verses of "How Great Thou Art" when the pastor stands up and asks everyone to bow their heads. Then, to your shock and amazement, he looks up into heaven and screams, "What the heck God! Wake up! We have been worshipping here for about thirty minutes, and now we can't even tell you are here. Are you sleeping or something?"

If ever a pastor had the guts to pray like that, the sound guy would immediately turn his microphone off and the deacons would drag him off the stage.

Hi, Marge, it's Alice. Did you hear what Pastor Bill did this week during the pastoral prayer? He told God to stop sleeping. Well, bless his heart, that's not very godly.

Needless to say, Psalm 44 is a long way off from the prayers we often hear,

Dear and Beloved God and Father, we beseech thee to come near to thine house and to gird thine blessing upon thy thigh. For thou art true and good and right.

Listen, as of the twenty-first century, the word "art" is a noun.

Seriously, can you believe God allowed Psalm 44 to make it into the Bible? Frankly, if I were God, the Bible would have about twenty fewer Psalms in it. The point, of course, is that he is God; he has left that Psalm right where it is...and I am pretty sure he's planning on keeping it there.

So, let me clear the air right now. Does God sleep? No. In fact in another Psalm God clearly says, "he who keeps Israel will neither slumber nor sleep" (Psalm 121:4). So then, why is there a prayer where someone asks God to wake up? It sounds like a contradiction, doesn't it?

The Psalm is there for two reasons.

First, it is there because when we endure suffering, we are often tempted to believe the lie that God is far away, asleep, or just not listening. That's because we expect him to show up on our timetable, and he is quite content to show up on his timetable. The feeling of his absence leads us to believe he's not there at all—or perhaps he has better things to do than to help us out.

John Eldredge says this, "We don't believe the Scriptures because they don't seem to align with what we are feeling right now. It has frustrated the living daylights out of me to see people clinging to their agreements and unbelief because it is what they are feeling in the moment."[74]

Second, the Psalm is there because it is 100 percent acceptable to tell God exactly how you feel. Think about it. He knows you are suffering. He knows you are upset. And he knows you're secretly blaming him for all of your problems. So, you might as well go ahead and tell him. This kind of honest praying gets through. I have no idea why this works so well, but it does. Just tell God your problems; tell him about your cares; and tell him you're upset because you feel like he went on

---

74   John Eldredge, *Walking with God* (Nashville, TN: Thomas Nelson, 2010), 100.

vacation. If you feel guilty about sharing your pain with God, then use the Psalms. He wrote them, so use them. When you pray like that, God will listen. And even better, when you pray like that, he will change your heart.

Jesus himself was not immune to unanswered prayer. At times Jesus asked for something, and the Father said no. Worse, there were times Jesus asked for something, and the Father simply said nothing. Can you imagine the pain Christ must have felt when the Father remained stoically silent? Here was a man who, for most of his human life, experienced unbroken communion with God the Father. Then, he came to ask for a simple request and heard nothing except the faint sound of crickets.

Luke tells us the story, "And he withdrew from them about a stone's throw, and knelt down and prayed, saying, 'Father, if you are willing, remove this cup from me. Nevertheless, not my will, but yours, be done.' And there appeared to him an angel from heaven, strengthening him. And being in an agony he prayed more earnestly; and his sweat became like great drops of blood falling down to the ground" (Luke 22:41–44).

Jesus prayed so hard blood, instead of sweat, came out of his pores. He pleaded and begged and cried. What was the Father's answer?

Total silence.

It must have broken Jesus' heart.

This from Frederick Buechner:

Later in the garden where it was his own death he had to sweat out, we are told he sweated blood.

He said, "Father, if thou art willing, remove this cup from me" (Luke 22:42), and the cup was not removed from him presumably because the Father was not willing to remove it, and one suspects that the unwillingness of the Father may have been harder for Jesus to choke down than the cup itself was. Later it was harder still. By the time he had been hanging there for a while, he had no tears left to weep with and no more sweat, his tongue so dry he could hardly wrap it around the words which are among the few he ever spoke that people remembered in the language he spoke them in probably because having once heard them, they could never forget them no matter how hard they tried, and probably they tried hard and often: "My God, my God, why have you—" and then the Aramaic verb from an Arabic root meaning to run out on, leave in the lurch, to be the Hell and gone. "My God, my God, why hast thou forsaken me" (Matthew 27:46).[75]

The Father's silence in the garden may be the most shocking story in all of the Scriptures—more scandalous even then the death of God on the cross. We find our answer to God's apparent silence as we sit with Jesus in the garden. But to truly understand the nature of God's silence to our prayers, we must first really and truly believe that Jesus was a man, all man—100 percent human, flesh, bone, emotions, and foibles, right down to the time he accidentally left his

---

75   Buechner, *Telling the Truth*, 38-39.

zipper down. Once we see him as a man, we then can join him in the garden as he cried, grunted, and screamed to a God who simply seems as if he is sound asleep.

> Here we have the incarnate Son praying through his tears and not receiving what he asks. Jesus knew the burden of unanswered prayer. He really did want the cup to pass, and he asked that it would pass. "If you are willing" was his questioning, his wondering. The Father's will was not absolutely clear to him. "Is there any other way?" "Can people be redeemed by some different means?" the answer—no![76]

When you experience the silence of God coupled with the lies of the enemy, you have one choice and one choice only. It's the same choice Jacob made in the goat pasture. It's the same choice Joseph made in the jail filth. It's the same decision David made in the cave. And it's the same choice Jesus made in the garden.

You must choose to get up, brush yourself off, and get back into the fight. The entire battle is won when you reject the lie that God is far off and embrace the truth that he is near. The victory comes when you toss every shred of external evidence and choose instead to believe God cares deeply, passionately, and vehemently about every aspect of your suffering.

The following exercise has proven quite helpful for me. Try this, especially when you are discouraged. Grab a pen and a

76   Richard Foster, *Prayer* (London, UK: Hodder & Stoughton Ltd, 2008), 49.

piece of paper. Find somewhere quiet, and turn off your phone, radio, and TV. Then, simply pray this one question out loud:

Father, what lies am I believing about you?

Then, just listen. Whatever comes to your mind, write it down. Don't edit your answers and don't try to understand them. Write down whatever you hear, see, sense, or feel. Just write it down.

Once you have done that, simply pray this (out loud):

Father, I reject the lie [say the first thing you wrote down]. Father, I reject the lie [say the second thing you wrote down]...

Keep doing that until the list is complete. You will feel silly. You will feel foolish. And you will feel like it's not working. That is from the enemy so reject that as well.

Then, ask God this question out loud:

Father, what is true about you?

Same drill. Write down everything you hear, see, sense, or feel...no matter how strange or silly. Don't make any interpretations or judgments (at least not yet). Then simply say:

Father, I choose to believe you are [say the first thing you wrote down]. Father, I choose to believe you are [say the second thing you wrote down], etc....

What you believe about God will affect what you believe about...everything. Once you get clear about God, you will get clear about yourself.

The first time I asked God what lies I was believing about him, here is what I heard:

I am far away.

I am disappointed in you.

I am not close.

When I asked God what was true, here is what I heard:

I am near.

I love you.

You are strong.

And I am proud of you.

Oh, he is good. He is good indeed.

Victory over suffering often comes hand-in-hand with victory over your beliefs. The lies of the enemy when coupled with the silence of God have been enough to bring many a saint to the end of their faith. Don't let that happen to you. Do what Jesus did and reject every lie, especially when it feels like God is far off. Then, once you have done that, go to his Word for something good.

CHAPTER 22:
BELIEVE HIS WORD

ONCE YOU REJECT the lies, listen carefully to God's Word and do what he says. During suffering, there is precious little to cling to other than his Word. Frankly, it's almost impossible to figure out why you are suffering. You will know that later. In fact, the not knowing why is often a part of the suffering.

Believing God's Word was not just something Jesus told us to do; it was something he did. And if Jesus did it, it stands to reason we should too.

When Christ went to Calvary, he carried nothing with him except a cross and the Word of God. He didn't need anything else. Jesus already knew what the Father thought of him, and this encouragement alone was apparently enough to get him through the silence. Twice in the Bible, once at his baptism and once at his transfiguration, God the Father broke through the silence and spoke audibly, "This is my beloved Son, with whom I am well pleased" (Matthew 3:17; 17:5).

That must have been pure joy to Jesus' human heart.

The Father is pleased...with me.

So when the whip scourged his back for the thirty-ninth time, he must have raised his head briefly and whispered,

The Father is pleased...with me.

When the five-inch thorns pierced his forehead and one exited through his left eyebrow, he must have raised his head briefly and whispered,

The Father is pleased...with me.

When the nails pierced his hands and feet, he must have raised his head briefly and whispered,

The Father is pleased...with me.

When he struggled for breath for the millionth time...

When the crowd laughed at his naked, exposed body...

When the soldiers played a dice game under the Maker of the Universe...

When he cried out to the Father, pleading, grunting, and sucking in more blood than air...he must have raised his head briefly and whispered,

The Father is pleased...with me.

And when he finally took his last breath—that struggling, complicated last gasp of air—and gave up his spirit as his chin slammed on his chest, he must have raised his head in heaven—

all the heavenly hosts silent (for what could the angels say?)—and looked his Father in the eye. Then, the heavenly silence broken, he must have seen the Father's smile, felt the Father's wide hand, and heard the Father exclaim,

"THIS IS MY BELOVED SON, WITH WHOM I AM WELL PLEASED!"

And like the end of the symphony, only multiplied a million times over, there was utter silence for a few seconds, and then in unison heaven exploded into thunderous applause, which has lasted even until this very day.

Jesus our example endured the cross, despising the shame. He did it because he steadfastly refused to believe in any other voice than the Father's. If Jesus needed to rely on God's Word, then how much more do you? In this world, you will have suffering. That's pretty much a fact of life. It's what you do with the suffering that counts. And there is nothing more important than hearing, listening, and believing in the Word of God.

In his epic novel, *The Screwtape Letters*, C. S. Lewis pens the advice from one senior demon to his younger student. The human "host" hadn't heard the voice of God for a while, and he was tempted to believe God was not there or at least he wasn't listening. The elder demon's advice was, "Our cause is never more in danger than when a human, no longer desiring, but still intending, to do our Enemy's will, looks round upon a universe from which every trace of Him seems to have vanished, and asks why he has been forsaken, and still obeys."[77]

---

[77] C. S. Lewis, *The Screwtape Letters* (New York, NY: Time Incorporated, 1963), 40.

It is essential during suffering to spend time in God's Word and ask him to deliver specific Bible texts you can hold onto through the difficult time. Once you find those, make copies and put reminders everywhere. You will need them. Then, get one-on-one with God and ask him for some words of encouragement from his throne.

Learning to hear God's voice is a process, but it's something you can learn to do—like learning French. When you listen to the voice of God, more times than not, he will give you something to hold onto—and very often it links directly to the Bible texts he has already shown you.

Neil Anderson tells us, "We take every thought captive in obedience to Christ. We are not called to dispel the darkness—we are called to turn on the light."[78]

I don't know why it works this way, but one of the main results of suffering is a closer walk with God. We just tend to hold fast to him when things get tough. A lot of voices are out there—friends', family's, the enemy's, and yours. None of them can be completely trusted. But you can trust God's voice. That's why drawing near to God during this time is so very important.

I can attest to that fact through my own suffering. My family and I have been going through a particularly rough financial time over the last year. It has been tough sledding. And while nothing has changed in our financial condition, a lot has changed inside my heart and inside my wife's heart.

---

78   Neil Anderson, *The Bondage Breaker* (Eugene, OR: Harvest House Publishers, 2006), 121.

Last year at this time, I ran and managed up to seven different businesses. The income was incredible, and I was able to use that income to help a lot of good causes. However, over the last year, and by God's specific leading, I shut down three business ventures entirely to make room for writing this book and for speaking on the topic of being a warrior for Christ. That decision was met with significant financial loss. To put it bluntly, my income was cut to about a fifth of what it was last year.

That hurt. That hurt a lot.

So for the last year, my family and I have been living week-by-week and waiting for God to provide. It has been one of the most difficult times of my life, but the results have been worth it.

I used to stay awake at all hours of the night worrying about money, bills, and taxes. My wife used to "mentally pack the house up and move to an apartment." I am glad to say that after a year, we are both sleeping better and we're not worried about money as much anymore. The situation didn't change—we changed. God skillfully used this situation to weave a deep and abiding trust in his heart and in his provision. I can honestly say I never wanted this kind of suffering, but I am truly thankful for it.

My recovery started with God's Word. One day, during a hike, I was pouring my heart out to God. Between you and me, I was angry. The money was gone, and I was pouting like a three-year-old. It was right then God, in his still small voice, said,

I will take care of you.

I honestly thought I was making things up to feel better, a sort of spiritual head trip. That's when I asked God for some specific verses to back up his promise. The following words popped out of the pages of my Bible: "I have spoken, and I will bring it to pass; I have purposed, and I will do it" (Isaiah 46:11).

I asked, "When, Lord? I know you will come through, but when?" I flipped through some more of my Bible and these words popped off the page: "I am the LORD; in its time I will hasten it" (Isaiah 60:22).

Another day, I was praying on the beach. I asked God again if he was really going to take care of us. He said,

I will take care of you. Love provides.

Another day, he took me to the passage in Genesis 22 that tells the story of Abraham's sacrifice of Isaac—the first place God calls himself "Yahweh Jireh," The Lord Who Provides.

All I can say is this: the evidence of God keeping his promise has been overwhelming. I am not exaggerating when I say several times we were simply out of money. I figured we would need a sizeable loan or to sell our house or to move to a different city.

And yet, every time, when just on the edge of despair, God came through.

Sometimes it was a paid speaking event that came out of the blue. Other times it was a past-due check that came right in the nick of time. Sometimes, well sometimes, the money just appeared. It occurred so often and so timely I started taking pictures of the checks and filing them in a folder called, "Crazy Things God Did."

How in heaven's name could anyone invent what has happened to us? Hollywood can't write stories better than this. We have literally experienced wave after wave of "just-in-time blessing" greater in magnitude than any "head trip" could ever produce. It's been almost a year, and we still have not missed a bill. It's been touch and go for sure. Not everything got paid on time, and we have had to clamp down on our spending. But, even with all that, we have still been able to give generously. We still buy the more expensive organic food and all natural milk for our family. We still have a date night every week or so. And I still get to make a batch of home-brewed beer and watch UFC every once in a while too.

During this difficult time, I battled accusation over my sin. I battled former business partners for monies due me. I battled health attacks on my family. I battled attacks against my character. And I battled discouragement. I have failed many times, but more times than not, I have simply rested on that simple promise:

I will take care of you.

And that's because when God says he is going to do something, he does it. Period. His word is sure. He doesn't change his mind, and he doesn't go on vacation. There is nothing (and I mean nothing) like the Word of God to get you through suffering. And what was true for Christ is doubly true for you and me.

There are times, to be sure, when it seems like God is all but gone. He does that on purpose, you know. He uses suffering to strengthen our faith in his promises. When we choose to obey him in suffering, even when it feels like he is long gone, the enemy will be defeated and we will win.

CHAPTER 23:

FOCUS ON THE RESULT, NOT THE SUFFERING

GOD WANTS TO bless you. He really does. And part of his blessing for your life is to train you to fight through suffering. That's why James said, "Count it all joy, my brothers, when you meet trials of various kinds, for you know that the testing of your faith produces steadfastness. And let steadfastness have its full effect, that you may be perfect and complete, lacking in nothing" (James 1:2–4).

Admit it. If you are like me, you secretly think James was smoking crack when he wrote that verse. Consider it a duty, yes. Consider it a privilege, maybe. But consider it joy? Are you out of your mind?

"Hi, Ted, how is the chemotherapy going?"

"Wow, Hank, thanks for asking. It's been nothing but joy. Joy, joy, joy. I throw up a lot...and that's always fun. I don't sleep at all, but then again I love being tired. And the left side of my head is bald, which makes me quite a hit with the ladies, you know!"

But then again, this is God's world and not ours. He is the one who makes the poor rich, the lame walk, the blind see, and the fools wise. He is the God of contradictions. Just when we have him in our careful little system, he shows us our system never worked in the first place. Just when we have him in a neat little box, he explodes the box, leaving shrapnel in our eyes.

And so yes, joy. Pure joy. Overwhelming, exciting, ecstatic, I can't-believe-this-is-happening-to-me joy. Joy like a seven-year-old girl dressed as Cinderella on Disney's Main Street USA. Joy like her five-year-old brother getting his first bike—with pirate stickers. Joy like his three-year-old brother waking up on Christmas morning.

Joy, joy, joy, and more joy, overflowing and never-ending.

Do you want to know why?

It's not because of what's happening *now*. It's because of what is going to happen. Through the suffering, he is making you stronger than Sampson, David, and William Wallace put together. He is building your spiritual muscles for endurance.

God has a mission for you, and it is going to take every ounce of strength to accomplish that mission. So God, in his infinite wisdom, is sending you through boot camp so when you come out on the other end, you will look at your newly formed Christian faith, character, and endurance and proudly say,

"Earned! Never Given!"

Henri Nouwen tells us about the heart of the Father in suffering, "Here is the Father God I want to believe in: a Father who from the beginning of creation, has stretched out his arms in merciful blessing, never forcing himself on anyone, but always waiting; never letting his arms drop down in despair, but always hoping that his children will return so that he can speak words of love to them and let his tired arms rest on their shoulders. His only desire is to bless."[79]

So, trust him, OK? He does everything for a reason, and you can bet your bottom dollar he has a very good reason for your suffering. You might never know the reason for your suffering, which is why Charles Spurgeon is often quoted as saying, "If you can't trace God's hand, trust his heart." If you can't even find the strength to trust him, then start by asking for that.

I gave a two-hour talk last month to a group of Christian business owners. Unbeknownst to me, in the crowd was a woman who had just been diagnosed with breast cancer. That

---

79   Henri Nouwen, *The Return of the Prodigal Son* (London, UK: Darton Longman and Todd, 1994), 95-96.

morning God told her she was his warrior. An hour later, one of the other speakers (not knowing about her cancer or about what God told her) said that he thought she was a warrior. That afternoon, I spoke on being a warrior. (Note: often God speaks in many different ways to send the same message.)

After the talk, she came up to me and said, "Ed, you don't know this, but I was diagnosed with cancer four days ago. And to be honest, I am very excited about what God is doing. I think one of two things is going to happen: either God will heal me or he will allow me to suffer so I can be an example to others as to what a warrior should be like during suffering."

I take off my hat. This is the kind of faith that could tell a mountain to jump into the ocean. This woman clearly understood God's purposes in suffering are always, always, always good.

So one of the keys to enduring suffering as a good soldier is to set your eyes on the result of your suffering and to know the Father has a good purpose for what he is doing. Once you know that, start praying for breakthrough. And then pray again. In fact, pray until you can finally come to him and say,

God, you know what I want. I have prayed for this a hundred times—maybe a thousand. So, I don't even think I need to say it again. Just come.

And then pray again.

Eventually, your suffering will be gone. Eventually, joy will replace sadness. Eventually, endurance will replace weakness. Eventually, the fog will lift, the pain will end, the trial will be over, and the bell will ring announcing the end of the fight.

Eventually, you will win.

CHAPTER 24:
EASE OTHERS' SUFFERING

YOU HAVE HEARD the song that goes, "Man of Sorrows, what a name! For the Son of God who came."[80] Here is the point: whatever you may be experiencing right now pales in comparison to what Christ experienced. Truly he bore our sorrows. Truly he carried our shame. Truly he suffered more than any man has ever suffered.

Even then, truly, in the midst of a pain so deep it would kill any one of us, he also chose to ease others' suffering. Jesus

---

80   Philip Bliss, "Hallelujah! What a Savior!", 1875 (Public Domain).

- 247 -

helped others during his time of suffering for at least two reasons. First, it was in his character to serve, and so he did not stop when he was suffering. Second, he was giving us an example to follow.

Here are three (of many) occasions where Christ unselfishly helped others during his suffering.

Let's look first at Mary, his mother: "When Jesus saw his mother and the disciple whom he loved standing nearby, he said to his mother, 'Woman, behold, your son!' Then he said to the disciple, 'Behold, your mother!' And from that hour the disciple took her to his own home" (John 19:26–27).

Now imagine this. Jesus could barely breathe because to do so required him to push up on a nail driven right through the frail tendons in his feet. He could hardly see because there was caked blood, sweat, and someone else's dried spit on his eyelids. He could barely smell because his nose was swollen shut. And he could hardly hear because the noises were drowned out by the sulfurous cackling taunts of the evil one.

Yet, he cracked open his eyelids to look with compassion on his mother, and he cracked open his mouth to ease her pain.

This was Mary—the same woman who heard the angel Gabriel say Jesus would be great. *Where is that greatness now,* she thought, *and for that matter, where is that angel?*

This was Mary—the same woman who heard twelve-year-old Jesus say he must be about his Father's business. *How can this be his Father's business,* she thought, *and for that matter, where is the Father?*

This was Mary—the same woman who heard Jesus on the cross say, "John, take good care of my mom. She needs you now. And for that matter, you need her too."

I am stunned as I witness this scene. That's because I immediately see how very un-Christlike I am in my suffering. One of my biggest revelations recently has been how selfish I am during suffering. My journals are full of prayers to God about what I want. However, sadly, precious few journal entries are about what others need. It's humbling to say the least.

Jesus, on the other hand, while in the midst of suffering so horrible just the thought makes you wince, chooses to spend one of his very last breaths to take care of two people who needed him in their suffering. It is truly one of the most remarkable, most courageous, most unselfish moments in history.

Next, let's look next at the soldiers, the rulers, and the crowd.

> Two others, who were criminals, were led away to be put to death with him. And when they came to the place that is called The Skull, there they crucified him, and the criminals, one on his right and one on his left. And Jesus said, "Father, forgive them, for they know not what they do." And they cast lots to divide his garments. And the people stood by, watching, but the rulers scoffed at him, saying, "He saved others; let him save himself, if he is the Christ of God, his Chosen One!" The soldiers also mocked him, coming up and offering him sour wine and saying, "If you are the King of the Jews, save yourself!" There was also an inscription

over him, "This is the King of the Jews." (Luke 23:32–38)

Let's face it—if anyone deserved swift and immediate punishment from the hand of God himself, it was the soldiers, the rulers, and the crowd.

The soldiers treated all this as a game—another criminal whose only worth was another set of clothes to sell on eBay.

The rulers treated this as retribution. "You see! This is exactly what happens when you mess with the rightful kings of the Jews. Stay out of our way...or you're next!"

The crowd, well they only came along for the show—just another crucifixion and another chance to make fun of someone who couldn't possibly defend himself. "You think you are so special Mr. Clean-Out-the-Temple. We told you not to do that and now, look. You are finally getting what you deserve! King of the Jews, my nose. He saved others, but he can't save himself? Pathetic."

No, actually, he was getting what *they* deserved. The perfect Son of God; the Creator of Orion, the Big Dipper, and Pleiades submitted himself to the accusations, the jeers, and the jokes of a crowd whose very hearts were being simultaneously held together by the "word of his power."

He could have remained silent, you know. He could have simply thought to himself, *Laugh it up. I'll see you on judgment day.*

Instead, as an act of final, shocking contradiction, Jesus said, "Father, forgive them, for they know not what they do."

Here is the interesting thing: the soldiers, the rulers, and the crowd didn't even ask for Jesus' forgiveness, yet he still chose to forgive them.

Do you know how hard that is to do?

Actually, I'll bet you do. My guess is people are in your life who have hurt you deeply, and to make matters worse, they never even asked for your forgiveness. In fact, they never will. Perhaps your husband or wife cheated on you; your father abandoned you; your mother beat you; your co-worker maligned you; or your friend betrayed you. The examples are endless, so just fill in the blanks with your own pain.

You know this much: you are right and they are wrong. And yet somehow, you end up hurt and they get off scot-free. How is that fair? Well, it's not, and that's why when that happens, you must do exactly what Jesus did. No matter how difficult. No matter how right you are. No matter how much you want to punch them in the face. You forgive. You simply forgive. You give it to God and say along with Jesus, "Father, forgive them, for they know not what they do."

When you do that, when you can find the strength to forgive, you will find (wonder of wonders) the one who becomes free is you.

Finally, consider the thief on the cross.

One of the criminals who were hanged railed at him, saying, "Are you not the Christ? Save yourself and us!" But the other rebuked him, saying, "Do you not fear God, since you are under the same sentence of condemnation? And we indeed justly, for we are receiving the due reward of our deeds; but this man has done nothing wrong." And he said, "Jesus, remember me when you come into your kingdom." And he said to him, "Truly, I say to you, today you will be with me in Paradise." (Luke 23:39–43)

If there was anyone at Calvary who got exactly what he deserved, it was the thief. Think about it. He never defended himself. He never blamed his bad lawyer or the angry judge. He never made excuses. He was guilty and he knew it. He broke all the Ten Commandments and would do it again if he had the chance. He beat his wife and abused his kids. He lied, cheated, and stole. He even joined in on the first round of abuse toward Christ.

Then, as a final act of supreme inconsistency, he literally did the thing right for the first time in his life. He simply asked the King to remember him—and nothing more. He didn't promise perfect obedience, nor did he promise to sell his possessions and give to the poor. He had nothing to give—no time, no money, and no property. The only thing he had was the Man next to him and a few last breaths. Incidentally, it's the only thing we have too.

Christ's response is enough to make you want to dance. He looked the thief in the eye and told him there was a party that afternoon and he was invited. There would be wine, food, and song, and the thief was going to be Emmanuel's guest of honor.

Words cannot begin to plumb the depths of Christ's compassion. He was the most amazing, loving, and kind man who ever lived. As the song goes, "Oh, the deep, deep love of Jesus, vast, unmeasured, boundless, free!"[81] "The man of sorrows and acquainted with grief. The one with the cauliflower ear and the split lip. By whose swollen eye and ruptured spleen we are somehow healed. Who can put a word to him and who needs to?"[82]

Mary found a shoulder to cry on. The soldiers, rulers, and crowd found forgiveness. The thief found a home. And here is the most amazing, astounding part of it all: because Christ had compassion on others, you can too.

In your life, there are people who need compassion, and, frankly, most of them don't deserve it. Either way, the call is clear. When you're suffering, your job is to ease others' suffering. It doesn't make sense, but neither does God dying.

Paul tells us the mission of the warrior is to "be sober-minded, endure suffering, do the work of an evangelist, fulfill your ministry" (2 Timothy 4:5).

In other words, do your job.

Your King set the example. Now follow in his footsteps. Endure suffering. Reject the lies. Believe the Word. Focus on the result, not the suffering. And ease the suffering of others.

---

81   Samuel Trevor Francis, "O the Deep, Deep Love of Jesus", 1875 (Public Domain).

82   Buechner, *Telling the Truth*, 21.

Once you do that, you will receive the endurance to fight alongside the King. He is the Conqueror after all. And that will be the subject of our next section.

SECTION 7:

CHRIST
THE
CONQUEROR

SECTION 7:
CHRIST THE CONQUEROR

"Regardless how and when you believe we are going to be taken to Heaven, we must rid ourselves of the idea that Jesus is coming to rescue His church. That lie has dislocated many generations of revolutionaries from their purpose in the same way a joint is pulled out of place. It has put the Church into a defensive posture of occupation to protect what we have instead of positioning ourselves for the purpose of increase."[83]

— Bill Johnson

"You have made them a kingdom and priests to our God, and they shall reign on the earth."

— Revelation 5:10

---

83   Johnson, *Dreaming with God*, 167.

NOTHING IS AS enthralling as a movie with a climactic finish. Nothing is as exciting as a close game where the home team wins. And nothing is so moving as a war story where the good guys come out on top.

We love happy endings—it's in our blood.

Just think about some of the most popular movies of all time.

At the end of the *Star Wars* trilogy, Luke Skywalker faced off against the emperor. If you remember the scene, Luke simply dropped his light-saber, forcing his true father, Darth Vader, to make a choice. He could either watch his son die, or he could kill the emperor. He valiantly chose to save his son. The rebels won, and there was once again peace in the galaxy.

The movie *Hoosiers* is a story of a down-and-out sports team that made it to the Indiana state championship game. Against all odds, they won on a last-second shot.

In the movie *Shawshank Redemption*, Andy Dufresne was a man wrongly accused for the murder of his wife. He spent a lifetime in Shawshank prison under the watchful eye of the evil warden.

His friend Red told of his escape: "Andy Dufresne, who crawled through a river of [filth] and came out clean on the other side. Andy Dufresne, headed for the Pacific. Those of us who knew him best talk about him often. I swear, the stuff he pulled. It always makes us laugh. Sometimes it makes me sad, though, Andy being gone. I have to remind myself that some birds aren't meant to be caged, that's all. Their feathers are just too bright."[84]

The last scene of the movie captures Red and Andy meeting on a beach in the Pacific—the warden having killed himself weeks earlier.

The list of dramatic movie endings is, well, endless...

Roy Hobbs hit the last home run in *The Natural*. The Grinch returned all the toys in *The Grinch That Stole Christmas*. And Ebeneezer Scrooge became a changed man in *A Christmas Carol*.

But dramatic endings are not limited to movies. Think about some of the most-dramatic sporting events of all time.

Do you remember Dwight Clark and Joe Montana? It has been called "The Catch"—the winning fingertip touchdown reception in the 1982 NFC Championship American football game between the Dallas Cowboys and the San Francisco 49ers.

---

84   *The Shawshank Redemption*, directed by Frank Darabont (Beverly Hills, CA: Castle Rock Entertainment, 1994).

Do you remember U.S. gymnast Kerri Strug? She competed in the 1996 Olympics, fell on her first attempt at vault, and busted her ankle. With no chance of a substitution, she limped to the end of the runway for her second attempt, nailed the vault, landed on one foot, and scored a 9.712, giving the United States the gold. She needed the assistance of her teammates to get onto the medal platform.

Oh, but this one takes the cake.

Do you remember the 1980 USA hockey team? They defeated the unbeatable team of Russians. That's when sportscaster Al Michaels delivered his famous call: "Eleven seconds, you've got ten seconds, the countdown going on right now! Morrow, up to Silk...five seconds left in the game...*Do you believe in miracles? Yes!*"[85]

Their story was featured in the movie *Miracle*, and the victory was voted the greatest sports moment of the twentieth century by *Sports Illustrated*.[86]

Then there is African-American Jackie Robinson signing a major league contract with the Brooklyn Dodgers, Kirk Gibson's game one home run against the Oakland A's, Michael Jordan's finals shot, and Michael Phelps's eighteen gold medals.

Of course, let's not forget the military.

---

85   HBO Sports. *Do You Believe in Miracles?: The Story of the 1980 U.S. Hockey Team* (New York, NY: HBO Home Video, 2001).

86   http://listverse.com/2008/11/15/top-15-greatest-sports-moments-of-all-time/

First Sergeant Leonard Funk single-handedly pinned down ninety Germans in World War II. He actually had five men in his squad, but, as fate would have it, he was the only one with a working weapon. Funk killed twenty of the ninety Germans, and then the other seventy surrendered...to him! Funk told his men, "That was the stupidest thing I've ever seen!" He was awarded the Medal of Honor for his bravery.

Then there is Lieutenant William D. Hawkins who "waged one of the most furious one-man army assaults on enemy positions in the history of modern warfare"[87] on the island of Tarawa. Hawkins was injured and forced onto a stretcher. While being carried away on a stretcher, he jumped off and took out three more Japanese machine-gun pillboxes. His friend later remarked, "To say that his conduct was worthy of the highest traditions of the Marine Corps is like saying the Empire State Building is moderately high."[88]

Then there is MacArthur's return to the Philippines, the Allies' victory over Napoleon at Waterloo, the Union conquest at Gettysburg, and finally Washington's ultimate triumph over Cornwallis at Yorktown.

The point is simple: there is nothing with the power to move, inspire, and motivate the human heart quite like a last-minute victory that overcomes all odds. And do you want to

---

87   http://listverse.com/2010/02/19/10-astounding-actions-earning-a-medal-of-honor/

88   Andrew Anthony Bufalo, editor, *Hard Corps—Legends of the Corps* (Abilene, TX: S&B Publishing, 2004), 112.

know why? It's because God knew, as a warrior, you would need every ounce of strength you could get to face your enemy and win.

But unlike dramatic movies, sports, and war, God tells us ahead of time how the game ends.

The last book we will explore for warrior themes is Revelation. In it, the theme is "Jesus the Conqueror." Through studying Revelation we learn two things: first, Christ wins and reigns; second, you win and reign with him.

Let's take them in turn.

CHAPTER 25:
GOD WINS AND REIGNS

THE BOOK OF Revelation can be confusing. With graphic imagery such as dragons, crowns, seals, and trumpets, it is easy to get lost in the shuffle. Add to that the fact that today's church has gone mad with predictions about the "signs of the last age." It's all a sad distraction from the true message.

Listen; to understand Revelation, you must first understand it was a real letter written to real people in the first century AD. Our generation is so self-centered we really feel John was ignoring everyone who came before us. We secretly act as if he saw a vision, wrote it all down, and then sent it to the first-century churches with the following, now-lost letter:

> OK, listen up, you seven churches. I know Jesus gave me twenty-two chapters in this book, but you can pretty much forget everything after chapter four. That's because it's not for you. It's not for your kids either...or your grandkids. It was actually written for these people called Americans. They live something like two thousand years from now and they pretty much think they are both the center of the universe and the culmination of all history. This book is basically for them.

I wish I were joking.

I can remember a good friend of mine calling me during the Gulf War in 1991. She said, since the Iraqi oil wells were on fire, the sky in the world would become dark like it says in Revelation 6...

...and then the end would come.

I can remember other friends talking about how the ten crowns on the head of the beast in Revelation 13 represented the Soviet Union—because they were pretty bad. They predicted the "beast" (i.e., the Russians) would shoot nuclear missiles at the United States. Then, America would shoot back...

...and then the end would come.

I can remember when a radio personality got the idea Christ was coming back on May 21, 2011. He and his followers bought a bunch of billboards telling people the end of the world was in a week, so do what you need to do, but it's all going down. They rented stadiums around the world and sang "Kum-Ba-Yah" until midnight.

The suspense must have been unbearable. They waited... and waited...and waited...

...and nothing happened.

That must have been a bummer of a ride home that night.

"Dad, can I have my Legos back now?"

"Sorry, son, we sold those along with the house so we could afford to rent the stadium for the pre-rapture party."

Now, listen. I am not saying to not be prepared. What I am saying, however, is nowhere in the Bible have we ever been called to cleverly interpret the Scriptures in any other way than the Scriptures interpret themselves. And we clearly are not supposed to start inventing dates, or creating prophetic wall charts or countdown timers.

Jesus didn't even do that—and he was God! "But concerning that day and hour no one knows, not even the angels of heaven, nor the Son, but the Father only" (Matthew 24:36).

There once was a seminary student who spent three whole years studying eschatology (that's the study of the "last times"). The day before graduation, he went to the seminary gym to work out. There he spotted the school janitor with his Bible open to the book of Revelation.

The prideful young man strutted over and asked, "Sir, how can you, a janitor, possibly know what that book means?"

The janitor didn't even look up. He simply replied, "Well, that's pretty easy."

The student responded proudly, "Oh yeah, then tell me. What exactly does Revelation mean?"

With a smile, the old man simply said, "We win!"

So, forget, for a moment, the worthless debates over the date of the end times and join the janitor. The message in the book of Revelation is so simple we often miss it completely: we win. Frankly, it's quite an encouraging way to end a collection of books intended for the lost, lonely, and lacking. And the best part of all is it's true.

Let's read one of the first sections of the book of Revelation to see if we can get some sign of the victory.

> Then I turned to see the voice that was speaking to me, and on turning I saw seven golden lampstands, and in the midst of the lampstands one like a son of man, clothed with a long robe and with a golden sash around his chest. The hairs of his head were white, like white wool, like snow. His eyes were like a flame of fire, his feet were like burnished bronze, refined in a furnace, and his voice was like the roar of many waters. In his right hand he held seven stars, from his mouth came a sharp two-edged sword, and his face was like the sun shining in full strength.
>
> When I saw him, I fell at his feet as though dead. But he laid his right hand on me, saying, "Fear not, I am the first and the last, and the living one. I died, and behold I am alive forevermore, and I have the keys of Death and Hades." (Revelation 1:12–18)

The shining person with the golden sash—that's Christ. The guy falling at his feet—that's John. Now to put this in its proper context, you need to remember John spent three full years with Jesus on earth. He was so close to Christ his friends called him "the disciple who Jesus loved." John was pretty much Jesus' best friend—so much so that at the Last Supper, John was spotted lying down on Jesus' chest.

This vision of Christ came at least thirty years later. During all of that time, John and Jesus didn't miss a beat. They still talked with each other. They still walked with each other. And they still loved each other, a lot. In fact, John was in exile at the time he wrote Revelation for his very controversial firsthand stories of his friend Jesus. In other words, if there was anyone who could spot Christ in a crowd, it was John.

So, what did John do when he got his first glimpse of Jesus in heaven?

Jesus, it's you! Long time no see. Hey, how's heaven? Boy, I can't wait! Well, things are going great on Patmos. I haven't seen Peter for a while, but he writes me from time to time.

No, it's nothing like that.

When John saw Jesus Christ the Conqueror, every muscle in his body went completely limp and he fell to the ground with a thud. He was completely and totally undone. Jesus' opening line was the same line he always used when humans saw his resurrected body: "Fear not." He had to say that because John was trembling, cowering, and whimpering in dread.

Thus, the opening of the story of Revelation gives us the first clue about the end of our own story. Jesus is more powerful than we will ever know, and he is going to slay his enemies.

The clock is ticking...

Jimmy Chitwood grabs the ball for the final shot. Kerri Strug limps up to the vault. Roy Hobbs steps up to the plate.

The anticipation starts to build.

What happens next in Revelation is what is happening now—an all-out war—a slug-fest for the ground of planet earth. The forces of darkness, who once owned sway over the nations, are now in retreat, shooting, ducking, and cowering in the darkness. The church, with its restored humanity and new names, marches to the beat of the heavenly fife and drum. We fire away with the Word of God and with the power of faith. The clock keeps ticking on the final quarter, and everyone has the growing sense something big is about to happen at the end of this story.

And, of course, it does...

Then I saw heaven opened, and behold, a white horse! The one sitting on it is called Faithful and True, and in righteousness he judges and makes war. His eyes are like a flame of fire, and on his head are many diadems, and he has a name written that no one knows but himself. He is clothed in a robe dipped in blood, and the name by which he is called is The Word of God. And the armies of heaven, arrayed in fine linen, white and pure, were following him on white horses. From his mouth comes a sharp sword with which to strike down the nations, and he will rule them with a rod of iron. He will tread the winepress of the fury of the wrath of God the Almighty. On his robe and on his thigh he has a name written, King of kings and Lord of lords. (Revelation 19:11–16)

The passage literally needs no explanation. A five-year-old can understand this. That's because we instinctively know from watching a thousand movies that when the king shows up on his white horse, with his armies behind him, things are about to change.

When Christ the King shows up on his white horse, the war is pretty much over and the outcome certain. There really are only two more things for him to do, which is to conquer death and send the devil where he belongs. He will do that in the very next chapter: "and the devil who had deceived them was thrown into the lake of fire and sulfur where the beast and the false prophet were, and they will be tormented day and night forever and ever" (Revelation 20:10).

The clock stops, the ball goes in the hoop, the gymnast nails the vault, and the baseball clears the right field fence.

The enemy is finally defeated and sent somewhere from which he will never, ever escape.

Ever.

Hunger is now gone, and for that matter so is rape, incest, lying, loss, suffering, and pain.

In their place is...Perfection. Take a moment to soak in the beauty of your future,

Then I saw a new heaven and a new earth, for the
first heaven and the first earth had passed away,
and the sea was no more. And I saw the holy city,
new Jerusalem, coming down out of heaven from
God, prepared as a bride adorned for her husband.
And I heard a loud voice from the throne saying,
"Behold, the dwelling place of God is with man.
He will dwell with them, and they will be his
people, and God himself will be with them as
their God. He will wipe away every tear from their
eyes, and death shall be no more, neither shall
there be mourning, nor crying, nor pain anymore,
for the former things have passed away."

And he who was seated on the throne said,
"Behold, I am making all things new." Also he said,
"Write this down, for these words are trustworthy
and true." And he said to me, "It is done! I am
the Alpha and the Omega, the beginning and the
end. To the thirsty I will give from the spring of
the water of life without payment." (Revelation
21:1–6)

It's a new heaven and a new earth. How much better could
this get? Well, actually much better because we get to dwell
with God face-to-face, as friends for all eternity. Remember that
same man who carried the cross, hung on Calvary, and forgave
the thief? You get to take as many hikes with him as you want
down near the river. You get to eat, drink, laugh, and dream.
You get to ask him for anything you want, and he'll give it to
you. Anything.

God wins. I want you to sit with that for a moment. God wins. This one idea alone is enough to overcome a world of hurt, pain, and regret. If instead of an entire Bible, all we had were those two words, God wins, it would be enough to get us to the end. That's because not a single problem, concern, issue, struggle, or battle will continue after...

God wins.

Frankly, that's very encouraging news. It means the Kingdom will finally come in all its power and glory. It means your mission will be complete. It means you will receive massive doses of authority and power. It means your time will have come. And it means your suffering will have a definite and permanent end.

No wonder John gets to the end of the book of Revelation and exclaims, "Come, Lord Jesus, come!"

Oh, but you want to know the best part? It's so good, so utterly delightful, that the enemy has been working successfully for years to steal this away from the church.

The best part is when God wins, *you win.*

When God's kingdom comes and he reigns, you will also get a kingdom...and you will reign too.

CHAPTER 26:
YOU WIN AND REIGN

L ET'S GO BACK to Revelation 21. That's the chapter with verses about the new heavens and the new earth I just quoted. I purposely left off verse 7 because it is so cool I wanted to talk about it all by itself.

Here is the deal. We know one day the new heavens and the new earth will come and God will win. What we have forgotten, however, is who exactly owns this new heavens and new earth?

The answer may surprise you: "The one who conquers will have this heritage, and I will be his God and he will be my son" (Revelation 21:7).

That, my friend, is you. I know it doesn't feel like it right now, but you are the one who conquers. It's right there in Revelation 21. It's the whole point of the story, and it's the whole point of this book. Like the only son of the wealthiest man on the planet, you get it all.

It's so amazing the devil has been trying for two thousand years to steal this from the church. And to be honest, he has done a pretty good job of it.

Think about our modern-day concept of heaven. It is a joke. Clouds, angels, Peter, and ten thousand years of singing. It's all...wrong. It's all a lie.

Here is the truth.

First, it's not only heaven. It's the new heavens and the new earth.

Second, it's not a bunch of clouds with powerless little angels flitting all about. Clouds are what Jesus rides to come back out of heaven and angels are uber powerful.

Third, it's not Peter at the front gates. In fact, the Bible doesn't talk about the "front gates" at all.

Fourth, and this one is the worst distortion of them all, it never says we are going to be sitting around singing songs for ten thousand years. That comes from the end of the song "Amazing Grace," not from the end of the Bible. I heard John Eldredge once say, "ten thousand years of singing? That doesn't sound like heaven; it sounds like hell. A weekend in Maui is better than that!"

He's right, you know.

In the new heavens and the new earth, we will walk on real, tangible ground with real, tangible bodies. We will drink real water, wine, and fruit juice, and it will taste good. We will eat from a bountiful supply of foods the imagination cannot fathom. We will hug, kiss, dance, smile, and sing. We will go to the movies, watch the ball game, and cuddle together on the couch with a bowl of popcorn.

In other words, we will be human—just as we were meant to be.

So, let me ask you this question: who stands to gain ground by giving God's people a distorted view of heaven?

Answer: the deceiver. The devil is a liar, and his strategy goes like this, "The church will eventually win and I will be toast. So, let's slow the whole process down by making Christians think it's not going to happen that way at all. In fact, call the people at Hallmark. We need some clouds, harps, and fat little cherubs. That'll do the trick. They will never want to fight for that."

It's the same lie that makes my non-Christian friends not want to go to heaven.

Who wants to go to church for ten thousand years when church for one hour is a nightmare. No thank you. I'll take my chances with that other place. At least my friends will be there.

It is instructive that the only time you find harps is in Revelation 15: "And I saw what appeared to be a sea of glass mingled with fire—and also those who had conquered the beast and its image and the number of its name, standing beside the sea of glass with harps of God in their hands" (v. 2).

Who gets the harps? The ones who conquer. That's you.

Now, if you didn't pay attention to anything I have said, pay attention to this one thing. It's vitally important you get this. Otherwise nothing else will make any sense.

Do you want to know why God is teaching you to serve the Kingdom? Do you want to know why he is giving you a mission? Do you want to know why he is training you in authority and power? Do you want to know why he is teaching you timing. And for heaven's sake, do you want to know why he is bringing so much suffering into your life—all of those losses, heartaches, tears, and sleepless nights?

Do you want to know why he is calling you to rise up and fight as a warrior, to wage war against your enemies?

There is one very good reason, and we find it tucked away in Revelation: "You have made them a kingdom and priests to our God, and they shall reign on the earth" (Revelation 5:10).

The reason God is training you as a warrior is you are going to reign with him on this earth. In short, he is training you to rule.

God is going to give you an inheritance that will be yours forever, which will never spoil or fade. And what you learn here, right now on this fallen earth, is creating in you the character to reign in the unfallen Kingdom that will soon be yours.

I can't even find the words to describe this.

It is pure...majesty. What I just told you means...everything. It changes...everything.

When you understand this one point, you will never look at another situation in your life the same way again.

Think about your relationships: friends, family, co-workers, and peers. How much more meaningful does each and every conversation become when you know, one day, you will reign with God?

Think about your job. It may seem like nothing more than a way to make a few bucks and get to the weekend. But, how much more meaningful does each and every task, each e-mail, each sales call, and each customer service inquiry become when you know, one day, you will reign with God?

Think about your trials—the seemingly never-ending tests of your faith and patience. There are days, to be sure, you just want to throw in the towel, give up, and head to the bar for a cold one. But, how much more meaningful does each and every frustration, depression, and loss become when you know, one day, you will reign with God?

No conversation will be the same—no relationship, no job, no trial, and no mission. It all changes when you realize Christ the King is right now training you for battle.

Perhaps it's high time we started acting like it.

At the end of *The Last Battle, Chronicles of Narnia*, the children find themselves on the new earth. Here is their experience:

And as He spoke, He no longer looked to them like a lion; but the things that began to happen after that were so great and beautiful that I cannot write them. And for us this is the end of all the stories, and we can most truly say that they all lived happily ever after. But for them it was only the beginning of the real story. All their life in this world and all their adventures in Narnia had only been the cover and title page: now at last they were beginning Chapter One of the Great Story which no one on earth has read: which goes on forever: in which every chapter is better than the one before.[89]

My friend, what you are experiencing now is nothing more than your first few weeks of God's kingdom boot camp, or as C. S. Lewis says, "the cover and title page."

And so now it is time. It is time to arise as a warrior. It is time to fight. It is time to take back what is rightfully yours. It is time to restore what has been stolen, lost, and destroyed. It is time to retake the land. And, finally, it is time to send the enemy back where he belongs.

Joy, breakthrough, peace, and victory are on the other side of the battle. And, to be perfectly honest, what *will* you do without your freedom?

When you know you are going to reign with Christ, there is one and only one appropriate response: you fight.

So, I will leave you with this one challenge and this one call.

---

89   C. S. Lewis, *The Last Battle* (New York, NY: Penguin, 1965), 210-11.

The world waits longingly for the sons of God to arise and claim the land on behalf of the returning King. The abused, maligned, and mistreated wait for the coming of the Kingdom. The homeless, sightless, and faithless wait for you to exercise your authority and act boldly on their behalf. The world waits, lost and dying, for the church to finally shake off its petty disputes and fight, once again, for its true inheritance.

The only question I have left is the one with which I started:

Will you fight?

If your answer is yes (and I hope it is), then welcome to the Victorious Army of God. Your training has now begun.

Together, let's storm the field...and win our freedom.

THE DISCUSSION CONTINUES AT:

www.CalledToVictory.com

To book Ed Rush for a speaking engagement,
conference, or retreat, you may contact his office at:

support@CalledToVictory.com

619-292-2599

* fees available on request

You can follow, share, listen, join, or watch the
continuing message of *Warrior* at one of the sites below:

Facebook
http://www.facebook.com/EdRush

Twitter
https://twitter.com/calledtovictory

YOU CAN ALSO connect with Ed on Pinterest, Tumblr, and several other social media sites. Ed usually makes at least one big, public, embarrassing mistake per week (and usually more). That is often captured for posterity on social media, so it would be great if you followed, liked, shared, or pinned him.

BOOKS FOR REFERENCE

I RECENTLY READ ABOUT seven books from a popular Christian author. They were all quite good. Then, I read the books he referenced as sources. What I saw were the roots to the tree. You see, new ideas have a way of growing in the fertile ground of old ideas. Show me a successful author, and I will show you a glorious company of other authors behind him, giving inspiration to new ways of looking at old things.

We stand on the shoulders of giants.

In this book, I barely scratched the surface on several issues worth much deeper consideration. I would commend to you the following books for your continued reading. They are listed below in topical format.

Grace and Forgiveness

The Ragamuffin Gospel and *The Furious Longing of God* (Brennan Manning)

Manning is a former Franciscan priest and recovered alcoholic. He calls himself a "ragamuffin." His words come from long-fought battles. He speaks with a refreshing winsomeness and humility. If you are in need of the reminder God loves you, despite what you did last night, get Brennan's books and marinate in them.

Three Free Sins (Steve Brown)

This has to be the best title for a book I have seen in a long time. But don't get worried. It's not heresy and Steve isn't encouraging sin. What he does is show you how big God is and how very much he loves you. As a personal note, Steve Brown and the Word of God are dually responsible for yanking me out of a three-year spiritual depression that almost destroyed my faith. If you like audio, go to KeyLife.org and listen to Steve's daily radio show. It's worth the visit.

Prayer

Prayer (Richard Foster) and *The Way of the Heart* (Henri Nouwen)

I have heard people say they "labor in prayer." I used to do that and it stunk. Plus, it doesn't make any sense. That's because prayer can be as simple as talking to a friend. Have you ever watched newlyweds walking in a park, waiting on each other's words? It can hardly be called "laboring in discussion." Friends communicate. Good friends communicate deeply. If you can sit for an hour and share a good story with a friend, you can pray with God—period. So stop making it so complicated and relax with your King. He loves you a lot, you know. Foster's book *Prayer* is a must read. His ability to take hard concepts and make them easy to apply is notable. Nouwen's *The Way of the Heart* is a short discussion of the necessary disciplines of solitude, silence, and prayer. It might not sound like a lot of fun, but try it once and you won't turn back.

Walking Conversationally with God

Hearing God (Dallas Willard), *Walking with God* (John Eldredge), and *Practice of the Presence of God* (Brother Lawrence)

I can't believe we lost this. Heck, I can't believe I lost this. God is called "the Word." He has been speaking to us one-on-one since the day he met Adam in the garden. He spoke one-on-one with Abraham, Moses, David, Christ, and Paul. And he didn't stop speaking when the Bible was complete. This one error has been responsible for more Christian dullness than any other. Seriously, what would we call a father who wrote his son a book of instructions, gave it to him when he graduated from high school, and then never spoke to him again? A degenerate.

That's not God. Throughout Scripture and throughout the course of Christianity, God has been speaking. It stands to reason he has something to say to you too.

Anecdotally, an advance word from God has saved me multiple times from untold heartache and pain. And his guidance during suffering has been absolutely necessary for endurance. And so if you are not listening and hearing from God, give it a shot. You may be surprised at what happens.

Listening to God takes training, and that's why I recommend the books above. Willard's book *Hearing God* is quite a balanced primer on how God speaks and how we can hear from him. In *Walking with God*, John Eldredge literally lets you read his journal entries for one full year. It is a way to show you the different ways God speaks into the situations of our lives. Brother Lawrence's time-tested treatise *Practice of the Presence of God* is also not to be missed. He'll show you how to communicate with God during even the most mundane tasks, such as washing dishes.

Finding Your Calling and Mission

It's Your Call (Gary Barkalow) and
Desire (John Eldredge)

Every human being asks one basic question: "why am I here?" The cool thing about being a Christian is the question has a definitive answer—an answer specific to you. In the military, we never fight without first being given a mission. The same should be true for soldiers in God's Army. As I mentioned earlier, finding your calling usually means a battle, and that is why I recommend these references.

Gary Barkalow has been a friend and ally in my personal quest to find my mission. He is basically the most gifted man I know for helping believers find their true call. His book *It's Your Call* is the place to start. Gary also helped with the message of *Desire* because he worked with John Eldredge's ministry when the book was written. That book focuses on using your own desires as a kind of compass to finding your mission in life.

Fasting and the Spiritual Disciplines

Celebration of Discipline (Richard Foster) and
Spirit of the Disciplines (Dallas Willard)

I love that Richard Foster uses the word "celebration." That's because when you truly get serious about the spiritual disciplines of prayer, fasting, solitude, submission, worship, and guidance, you really can start to celebrate. It couldn't be more paradoxical, and it couldn't be more true. God designed you as a human with a certain set of switches that "turn on" your spiritual "game." All I can say is try it.

Gifts and Healing

The Healing Gifts of the Spirit and *The
Healing Light* (Agnes Sanford)

Agnes Sanford was a warrior. She was a well-known healer who had a humble ability to make things happen. She knew how to pray—and after all, what is healing but a simple answer to prayer? I honestly did not give much credence to miracles until I read these two books. But the truth is right in the pages of Scripture. God gives his people power to remake our world. Imagine what will happen when the church begins to get this.

Both books are great. *The Healing Gifts of the Spirit* discusses all of the biblical gifts while *The Healing Light* narrows the topic to healing prayer—with a lot of personal stories included.

Spiritual Warfare (Angels, Demons, and the Like)

Bondage Breaker (Neil Anderson), *Victory over
the Darkness* (Neil Anderson), and *Handbook
for Spiritual Warfare* (Dr. Ed Murphy)

I did not talk much in the book about hand-to-hand demonic combat. That's because, first, I am still learning to master this discipline myself. And, second, those books have already been written by far more competent authors than me. Needless to say, there is a spirit realm the evil side of which can do you much harm. To ignore this reality is to leave your flank open to great attack. We don't talk about this much today because we don't like to. But remember the saying, "The devil's greatest lie was to convince the world he doesn't exist." So don't obsess about spiritual warfare, but don't overlook it either. Both of Neil Anderson's books come highly recommended. They are the place to start. For more in-depth reading, Dr. Ed Murphy's *Handbook for Spiritual Warfare* is the definitive 600-plus-page volume on how to fight the darkness.

Dominion and Victory

Liberating Planet Earth (Gary North), *Ruler of the Nations* (Gary DeMar), *Institutes of Biblical Law* (R. J. Rushdoony), and *Dreaming with God* (Bill Johnson)

Christ is King—and he wants you to rule. If you have read this far, you know this already. The books above will take you much deeper into what it takes to rule well. The first two books are a part of the *Biblical Blueprint Series*, quite an effective collection on the topic of taking dominion.

Rushdoony's *Institutes of Biblical Law* is not for the faint of heart. It is close to 900 pages on the application of God's Word in today's world. It is very good but is limited to aspects of rule. That's why if you have a soft conscience, be sure to balance that reading with one of the books I recommended on grace.

Dreaming with God is excellent. Bill Johnson is quite an effective pastor, and he writes from his "in-the-trenches" experience. His Bethel Church is a prime example of the good fruit Christians yield when they start taking dominion. Parenthetically, I have also been greatly helped by Bethel's

"Sozo" inner healing ministry. Sozo is a way to connect one-on-one with God and achieve three years of healing in about two hours.

For Everything Above (and Everything Else)

The Bible (God)

I am not being trite here. God's Word is the most powerful, applicable, inspiring, and true book on the planet. Period. I am constantly amazed at how only one single passage, verse, chapter, concept, or story can fuel me with spiritual energy for days or even weeks. And when you couple God's Word with his indwelling Spirit, you can move mountains. Bible reading should be a daily activity (duh). But don't make it obligatory; instead, it should be fun and energizing. Start small. Read a chapter a day when you get up in the morning or when you get to work. Read another chapter at night. Read it to yourself, and read it to your family. Read it like your life depends on it—it does. Then let God do the rest.

Made in the USA
Lexington, KY
23 November 2012